JOHNSONVILLE
BIG TASTE OF SAUSAGE
COOKBOOK

Shelly Stayer
AND
Shannon Kring Biró

Johnsonville

BIG TASTE

OF

Sausage

COOKBOOK

Broadway Books   New York

PRINTED IN THE UNITED STATES OF AMERICA

BROADWAY BOOKS and its logo,
a letter B bisected on the diagonal,
are trademarks of Random House, Inc.

Visit our Web site at www.broadwaybooks.com

Book design by Elizabeth Rendfleisch

Library of Congress Cataloging-in-Publication Data

Stayer, Shelly, 1962–
    Johnsonville big taste of sausage cookbook /
Shelly Stayer and Shannon Kring Biró.
        p. cm.
    1. Cookery (Sausages) 2. Johnsonville Sausage, LLC.
I. Biró, Shannon Kring. II. Title.

TX749.5.S28S73 2006
641.66—dc22

                                        2005058159

ISBN-13: 978-0-7679-2435-1
ISBN-10: 0-7679-2435-5

10 9 8 7 6 5 4 3 2

First Edition

To my mother, Arlene Reilly,
my role model as a woman in business.

And to my mother-in-law, Alice B. Stayer,
who worked behind a meat counter 365 days a year
to create the first Johnsonville customers.

SHELLY

Johnsonville founder, Ralph F. Stayer, enjoys a sweet moment of rest atop a pile of sugar sacks.

CONTENTS

FOREWORD

Sausage has been a part of my life for as long as I can remember. I love making it and I love eating it. We eat sausage almost every day. What you might find interesting is that my family and I are not alone. People take their sausage very seriously here in Wisconsin. It is said that we have three basic food groups here—beer, cheese, and brats. As you can imagine, people who are that serious are also very opinionated about how to cook them. Wisconsin grillers are divided into several camps: boil in beer before grilling, grill first and then put them in a tub of beer, butter, and onions, don't use beer at all, grill with the cover on, grill with it off, etc., etc. Then there is the condiment controversy.... This can be very confusing to a neophyte brat griller. The important thing to remember is that the best way to cook a brat, and the best way to eat it, is how you like it. Whenever anyone asks me, "What is the best thing to put on a Johnsonville brat?" my answer is always, "Your teeth." We have collected a lot of different sausage recipes over the years and have developed quite a few unique methods for preparing it. We receive hundreds of inquiries every week asking for cooking instructions or recipes. This book is our way of sharing them with you. Try them. Enjoy them, and start on your own journey through the wonderful world of great-tasting sausages.

That journey started for me when my parents, Ralph and Alice Stayer, bought a little meat market in Johnsonville, Wisconsin, in 1945. They moved up from Milwaukee to start their own business and take their shot at living the "American Dream." This was quite a change for them. Johnsonville was and is a very small hamlet in the German farming country of eastern Wisconsin. The population was sixty-five people. The house they lived in was attached to the butcher shop, and it didn't have any indoor plumbing. I was two years old at the time, and in my distant memory, I can still picture myself bathing in an old copper washtub. Everything, even an empire, has to start somewhere, and this was the birthplace of what is now the leading sausage manufacturer in the United States.

In every business success story, someone sees a need and then finds a way to satisfy that need profitably. Ours began with bratwurst. Shortly after they arrived, my parents attended several functions where brats and hamburgers were grilled and sold to raise money for local charities. My dad noticed that there were many partially eaten brats thrown away in trash containers. He decided on the spot to focus on making a great-tasting brat so people would buy another rather than throw the first one away. At the time, hamburgers outsold brats five to one at these events. He knew he was successful within a year, because brats were outselling hamburgers five to one at the same events. To this day, we haven't changed the recipe. By the way, there are only two people in the world who know that recipe—my dad and I.

Johnsonville is a town of only sixty-five people. It wasn't big enough to support a sausage business, so my parents used their growing reputation for excellent sausage to open three retail markets in neighboring communities. This provided them with a good living, and things remained the same until I joined the business after graduating from the University of Notre Dame in 1965. By then, we had a very good local reputation, so I started selling and delivering to other food stores in the area. This worked so well that in 1968 we formed two companies—one for retailing and the other for manufacturing and wholesaling.

The manufacturing business experienced steady growth within the state of Wisconsin for the next decade, and then we decided to spread our wings outside the state. We would like to tell you that we made a very astute busi-

ness assessment regarding the right market in which to begin our interstate operations. We'd like to, but that wouldn't be true. My sister, Launa, lived in Fort Wayne, Indiana, and she wanted to join the company, so we decided to start there—so much for strategic business planning. She became our first out-of-state salesperson. We did so well there that we rapidly expanded into other markets in the Midwest and then outward from there. Since the late 1990s, we have been selling our sausage in every state in the union.

Along the way, brats have become one of America's favorite grilling foods. This is thanks in large part to Wisconsin expatriates who lived in the new markets we entered. For years, they would take brats back home with them after a visit to Wisconsin or have friends or relatives ship brats to them. Then they would invite friends over and have what we call locally a "brat fry." By the time our products got into distribution in those markets, there was a base of customers waiting for us. They would find the brats in the stores and send us thank-you letters. We have gotten thou-

"Miss Sheboygan JC" represented 1958's Brat Days. Nearly a half century later, the local Jaycees organization continues to host Brat Days.

Foreword

sands over the years. Frankly, it is we who should be thanking them, because they certainly paved the road for us.

Our people have worked extremely hard to create national awareness for this local delicacy. We celebrate our successes in a unique way. When we obtain distribution in an important supermarket chain in a new market, the salesperson calls in to Johnsonville and gets me on the phone to report the good news. I get out a firecracker and shoot it off in my wastebasket. We have gone through quite a few wastebaskets in the last twenty-five years. Now that we are in every chain in this country, we use firecrackers to celebrate sales breakthroughs in other countries and for innovations that make our products better.

Speaking of other countries, we are now selling our products in over forty countries. We have been working to build our international business for ten years and are making a lot of progress. When we first started, we thought we would have to create different flavors for some other countries. We couldn't imagine that people in Asia or other parts of the world would like the same sausage that we like. We were fully prepared to develop new flavors for them. Imagine our shock when we learned that they loved our brats just the way they were. We have created products for local tastes as well, but our original brat is still the best seller in every international market we are in.

It is amazing how much you can accomplish when you are doing something you love to do. It has been sixty years since the copper washtub, and forty years since I graduated from college. Some people might call that a career, but for me it's a prelude. There is still so much to do. We want to share the great taste of Johnsonville sausage with the rest of the world. Our goal is to make Johnsonville the Coca-Cola of sausage. It's a lofty goal, but we don't have anything else on our schedule for the next forty years, so why not?

Ralph C. Stayer

ACKNOWLEDGMENTS

We wish to thank Ralph C. Stayer, a luminary who graciously shared early stories of hard work and determination. Your continued striving to be the best sausage maker in the world has yielded one of the great American success stories.

Ralph F. Stayer, who spent countless hours butchering so that Johnsonville could become what it is today.

Tony Rammer, Johnsonville's art director, who provided guidance, brand expertise, and much-appreciated enthusiasm. You *are* Johnsonville.

Mike Zeller, who lent us his culinary expertise and plenty of laughs along the way. Your hard work in the kitchen is the backbone of these recipes.

Dori Fors and Heather Blamey, whose research, transcriptions, and administrative support allowed us to focus on writing. Natalie Kring, whose last-minute editing prowess has once again impressed her big sister.

Those who provided us with invaluable feedback on the recipes: Stephanie Bird, Sharrol Butzen, Sharon Cook, Sue Danneker, Mary Dotz, Kathy Fischer,

The local men give the streets new names in preparation for 1954's Brat Days celebration.

Joan Frye, Pat Gallagher, Joanne Gohr, Gretchen Hansen, Heidi Huberty, Jennifer Kluge, Kathy Kremer, Kara Lichtenberg, Paula Mayer, Carrie Niedert, Denise Nieland, Janet Steffensmeier, Joe Steffensmeier, and Tammy Strebe.

And last but certainly not least, those who ensured that this book became a reality: Broadway Books' Jennifer Josephy and Kristen Green, who have given us the perfect balance of autonomy and encouragement; Cathy Fowler of Redwood Agency, who nurtured this project from start to finish; and Shimon and Tammar, whose work and spirit are an inspiration.

JOHNSONVILLE
BIG TASTE OF SAUSAGE
COOKBOOK

By 1954, the Johnsonville Sausage staff had already grown.

START THE DAY
the *Johnsonville* WAY

APPLE SAUSAGE PANCAKES

CINNAMON BREAKFAST BAKE

VERMONT MAPLE SYRUP BREAKFAST PIZZA

APPLE AND SAUSAGE CRÊPES FOSTER

JOHNSONVILLE HASH BROWN BREAKFAST PIZZA

APPLE SAUSAGE BISCUIT BREAD

EGG AND SAUSAGE STRUDEL

CHEESY BREAKFAST WRAPS

SOUTH OF THE BORDER BREAKFAST TORTILLAS

BROWN SUGAR & HONEY BREAKFAST WRAPS

FRUIT AND NUT COMPOTE WRAPS
WITH BROWN SUGAR & HONEY SAUSAGE

WAKE-UP FRITTATA

SUNRISE BREAKFAST CASSEROLE

SAUSAGE AND MUSHROOM QUICHE

SAUSAGE AND EGG TURNOVERS

CAJUN "BY YOU" BREAKFAST

JOHNSONVILLE BREAKFAST EMPANADAS

SWEET SUGAR PIGLETS IN HONEY BLANKETS

APPLE *Sausage* PANCAKES

This recipe is especially fantastic in the fall, when fresh-picked Granny Smith apples are available in their crispest, most flavorful glory. You may substitute the apple of your choice, but crisp, slightly tart varieties such as Pink Lady and Golden Delicious best balance the juicy sweetness of Johnsonville Brown Sugar & Honey Links.

Cinnamon-flavored applesauce works well in place of the apple butter. We like using buttermilk pancake mix in this recipe, but you may wish to use a buckwheat or whole wheat mix. SERVES 8

TOPPING
One 12-ounce package
   Johnsonville Brown Sugar
   & Honey Links
$1/4$ cup unsalted butter
$3/4$ cup packed brown sugar
$1/4$ cup honey
$2^1/4$ cups peeled and cubed
   Granny Smith apples
$1/4$ cup apple butter

PANCAKES
2 large eggs
1 cup milk
2 cups pancake mix
1 tablespoon cinnamon
3 Granny Smith apples,
   peeled and grated
$1/2$ cup pecans, toasted

1. Preheat the oven to 375°F.

2. To make the topping: Place the sausage on a baking sheet and bake for 10 minutes. Turn once, and then bake for an additional 5 to 10 minutes, until the sausage is no longer pink. Drain the sausage, reserving about 1 teaspoon of the fat for brushing. Bias-cut the sausage into $1/2$-inch pieces.

3. In a heavy saucepan, melt the butter over medium-high heat. Stir in the brown sugar and honey; bring to a boil, stirring constantly. Add the apples and apple butter. Return to a boil. Reduce the heat to low, and simmer until the apples are tender, 3 to 5 minutes. Add the sausage and heat through, about 1 additional minute. Remove the pan from the heat, and cover to keep warm.

4. To make the pancakes: In a large bowl, beat together the eggs and milk. Stir in the pancake mix and cinnamon until moistened. If the batter is too thick, you may need to add another drop or two of milk. Fold in the apples.

5. Heat a griddle. Brush the surface with the reserved fat to prevent sticking. Using a 4-ounce ladle, about $1/2$ cup, pour the pancake batter in pools that are 2 inches away from one another. When the pancakes have bubbles on top and are slightly dry around the edges, in about $2^1/2$ minutes, flip them over. Cook until golden on the bottom, about 1 minute.

6. Serve the pancakes with dollops of the topping. Sprinkle with the pecans, and serve immediately.

— CINNAMON *Breakfast* BAKE —

This is one of the simplest, most delicious breakfast recipes you'll ever try. For variation, you may wish to drizzle the finished dish with warm honey before serving. SERVES 4

One 12-ounce package
  Johnsonville Brown Sugar
  & Honey Links
12 slices white bread
One 21-ounce can apple-pie
  filling
12 large eggs, lightly beaten
1½ cups milk
1 tablespoon cinnamon
1 tablespoon vanilla

1. Preheat the oven to 350°F.

2. Prepare the links according to the package instructions. Allow to cool slightly. Slice into ¼-inch coins.

3. Cube the bread and place it into a greased 9-by-13-inch pan.

4. In a large bowl, combine the pie filling, eggs, milk, cinnamon, vanilla, and sausage coins. Pour this mixture over the bread, making certain that the apples and sausage are distributed evenly.

5. Bake for 35 to 40 minutes, until the eggs are set. Let stand 10 minutes before slicing.

—VERMONT *Maple Syrup* BREAKFAST PIZZA—

Pizza for breakfast? You bet. Fluffy scrambled eggs, mouth-watering Vermont Maple Syrup Links, and thick and chunky salsa are placed on a prebaked pizza crust, then covered with mozzarella cheese that bakes up bubbly and golden brown. You may wish to add sautéed green bell pepper, onion, or mushrooms for extra flavor and color.

SERVES 4

One 12-ounce package Johnsonville Vermont Maple Syrup Links
One 16-ounce jar thick and chunky salsa
One 12-inch prebaked pizza crust
3 eggs, scrambled
4 ounces mozzarella cheese, shredded

1. Prepare the links according to the package instructions. Drain and slice.

2. Preheat the oven to 450°F.

3. Spread the salsa evenly over the pizza crust. Place the eggs evenly over the salsa, and cover with the sliced links.

4. Sprinkle the cheese evenly over the pizza, and bake for 8 to 10 minutes, until the cheese is melted and golden brown.

Apple and Sausage
CRÊPES FOSTER

This is our take on the traditional crêpes Foster. Instead of bananas, we use a scrumptious blend of brown sugar, honey, Granny Smith apples, apple butter, juicy Johnsonville Brown Sugar & Honey Links, and apple liqueur. Topped with cinnamon, confectioners' sugar, toasted pecans, and pomegranate seeds, Apple and Sausage Crêpes Foster also makes a heavenly dessert.

Cornstarch slurry is used to thicken sauces, gravies, pie fillings, and puddings. It is made by whisking together equal parts cornstarch and a cold liquid, such as water.

SERVES 4

13 Johnsonville Brown Sugar & Honey Links

CRÊPES
1 1/2 cups all-purpose flour
1 teaspoon salt
2 cups milk
4 large eggs

FILLING
1/4 cup plus 3 tablespoons unsalted butter
3/4 cup brown sugar
1/4 cup honey
2 1/2 cups peeled and diced Granny Smith apples
1/4 cup apple butter
1/4 cup cornstarch slurry (see headnote)
1/2 cup Calvados or other apple liqueur
1 teaspoon cinnamon
1/4 cup granulated sugar
1/4 cup confectioners' sugar
1/2 cup pecans, toasted
1/2 cup pomegranate seeds

1. Prepare the links according to the package instructions. Allow to cool slightly. Slice into 1/4-inch coins.

2. To make the crêpes: In a medium bowl, mix together the flour and salt.

3. In a large bowl, gently whisk together the milk and eggs. Gradually add the flour mixture to the egg mixture, stirring until it becomes smooth. Let stand at room temperature for 1 hour, so that the flour swells and the air beaten into the batter dissipates. If the batter becomes too thick, add a bit more milk.

4. Heat an 8-inch nonstick sauté or crêpe pan over low heat. Pour 2 tablespoons of the batter into the pan, lifting and tilting it to spread the batter evenly. Cook until golden brown around the edges, about 30 seconds. Gently flip the crêpe, and cook for another 30 seconds. Invert onto paper toweling. Repeat with the remaining batter, making 16 crepes total.

5. To make the filling: Melt $1/4$ cup of the butter in a medium saucepan over medium heat. Add the brown sugar and honey. Bring to a boil, stirring constantly. Boil for 1 minute. Add 1 cup water, the apples, and apple butter. Allow to simmer for 3 minutes, stirring occasionally. Add the sausage and slurry. Cook, stirring frequently, until the liquid is the consistency of honey.

6. Place 2 tablespoons of the filling on one-quarter of each crêpe. Fold in half, and then in half once again, so that the crêpes resemble triangles.

7. Place a bit of the remaining butter into a medium sauté pan and melt over medium heat. Place four crêpes into the pan, and carefully drizzle with 2 to 3 tablespoons of the liqueur. Cook for 30 seconds on each side. Repeat with the remaining crêpes, adding more butter as necessary.

8. Serve sprinkled with the cinnamon, granulated sugar, and confectioners' sugar. Garnish with the pecans and pomegranate seeds.

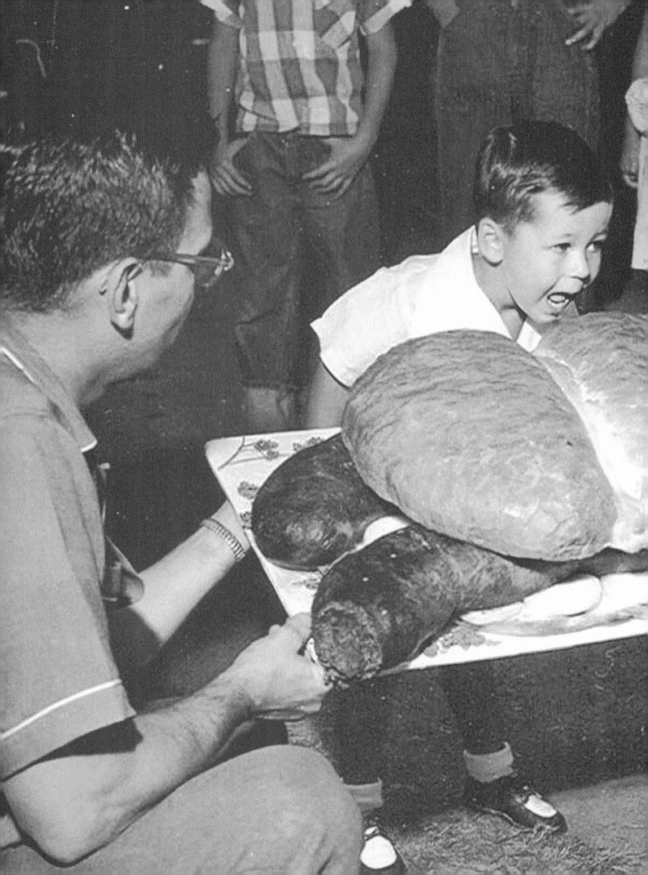

For father and son, two brats are better than one!

Johnsonville Hash Brown
BREAKFAST PIZZA

This tasty pizza is made with a buttery, flaky crescent-roll crust, rather than a traditional pizza crust. It's so good you just may start preparing it for dinner! SERVES 8

One 12-ounce package
   Johnsonville Original
   Breakfast Sausage Links
One 8-ounce cylinder
   refrigerated crescent rolls
1 cup refrigerated or thawed
   frozen hash-brown
   potatoes
1 cup shredded Cheddar
   cheese
4 large eggs
1/4 cup milk
1/4 teaspoon dried basil
Cayenne pepper
1/2 cup grated Parmesan
   cheese

1. Preheat the oven to 375°F.

2. Place the links in a baking pan. Bake for 15 to 20 minutes, turning once, until they are no longer pink. Drain, and slice into 1/2-inch coins.

3. Unroll the dough, and separate the sheets where perforated. Place the triangles with the points facing the center on a 12-inch pizza pan. Using your fingers, press the seams together and push the dough to the edge of the pan, making certain there are no gaps or holes.

4. Place the potatoes on top of the dough. Top with the sausage and Cheddar cheese.

5. In a medium bowl, whisk together the eggs, milk, basil, cayenne, and Parmesan cheese. Pour this mixture over the pizza-crust dough, and bake for 20 to 25 minutes, until the cheese is melted and a knife inserted near the center of the pizza comes out clean.

Our Favorite Ways to Prepare 'Em

The only thing worse than waking up on the wrong side of the bed is starting the day without the irresistible flavor of Johnsonville breakfast sausage links. Ensure happy mornings by preparing them the Johnsonville way.

Thaw Johnsonville Vermont Maple Syrup Links or the breakfast links of your choice thoroughly before cooking. You may use your microwave for this.

Cook them in a preheated skillet over medium-low heat for 10 to 13 minutes, turning them over with tongs to brown them evenly. To prepare the links in the oven, place them on a sheet pan and bake at 375°F for 18 to 20 minutes. Turn them halfway through. Sausage is cooked thoroughly when it reaches an internal temperature of 180°F.

Refrigerate unused links by removing them from their tray and placing them in plastic wrap or in a resealable plastic bag. They'll stay fresh and flavorful for 1 to 2 days. You may freeze them for up to 30 days.

Reheat them in a microwave on high power for 1 to 2 minutes. Pan-heat them over medium heat for 3 to 5 minutes.

APPLE *Sausage* BISCUIT BREAD

This scrumptious bread is as easy as it is delicious, making it the ideal recipe to prepare with the kids. MAKES TWO 9-INCH LOAVES

One 12-ounce package
   Johnsonville Brown Sugar
   & Honey Links
2 tablespoons cinnamon
1 teaspoon granulated sugar
Four 7$^1/_2$-ounce cylinders
   refrigerated buttermilk
   biscuits
Two 21-ounce cans apple-pie
   filling
Confectioners' sugar for
   dusting

1. Preheat the oven to 325°F.

2. Place the links in a baking pan. Bake for 10 minutes, and then turn. Bake an additional 5 to 10 minutes, until the links are no longer pink. Drain and slice into $^1/_4$-inch coins.

3. In a shallow dish, combine the cinnamon and granulated sugar. Separate the biscuit dough, and dredge the biscuits in the cinnamon-sugar mixture.

4. In a large bowl, combine the pie filling and sliced links.

5. Arrange the biscuits in a row on their edges in two greased 9-by-5-by-3-inch loaf pans. Top with the filling-sausage mixture. Bake for 70 to 80 minutes, until the top of the loaves are golden brown. Allow to cool, and then dust lightly with confectioners' sugar. Refrigerate any leftovers.

— EGG AND *Sausage* STRUDEL —

You've probably heard of apple strudel, but did you know that strudels—the flaky, filled German pastries that bake up crisp and golden brown—could also be savory? This delicious strudel is filled with juicy Johnsonville Original Breakfast Sausage Links, mushrooms, onions, cottage cheese, and sharp Cheddar cheese. Breakfast doesn't get any better than this. SERVES 8

One 12-ounce package Johnsonville Original Breakfast Sausage Links

2 sheets frozen puff pastry, thawed

2 teaspoons unsalted butter

1 1/2 cups (8 ounces) sliced fresh mushrooms

1 medium yellow onion, sliced

2 garlic cloves, minced

Salt

Freshly ground black pepper

12 large eggs

3 tablespoons cottage cheese

6 ounces sharp Cheddar cheese, shredded

1. Preheat the oven to 400°F.

2. Prepare the links according to the package instructions. Slice them into 1/4-inch coins.

3. On a lightly floured surface, roll out the pastry sheets until they are 12 by 16 inches each. Place one sheet onto a nonstick baking sheet, and set the other pastry sheet aside.

4. In a medium nonstick pan, melt 1 teaspoon of the butter. Add the mushrooms and onion, and sauté until lightly golden, about 2 minutes. Add the garlic, and season with salt and pepper. Add the cooked sausage, and heat through.

5. Break the eggs into a medium bowl, add the cottage cheese, and lightly whisk together. Season with salt and pepper. *(continued)*

6. Melt the remaining butter in a large sauté pan over low heat and scramble the egg–cottage cheese mixture to your desired doneness. Sprinkle over the pastry sheet that was placed on the baking sheet. Top with the sliced links, mushrooms, onion, and Cheddar cheese. Cover with the remaining pastry sheet. Brush the edges of each sheet with water, and crimp together to seal.

7. With a sharp knife, pierce the strudel to create steam vents. Bake for 20 to 25 minutes, or until golden brown. Allow to cool slightly before slicing.

Cheesy Breakfast
WRAPS

Two 16-ounce packages
    Ground Johnsonville
    Sausage
1 tablespoon olive oil
1 tablespoon chopped garlic
$3/4$ cup sliced scallions,
    white and green parts
1 teaspoon freshly ground
    black pepper
$3/4$ cup diced red bell
    pepper
$1/3$ cup sliced black olives
12 large eggs
$1/4$ cup crumbled blue
    cheese
Twelve 12-inch tortillas
Three 8-ounce jars cheese
    sauce

Strapped for time in the morning? Cook the sausage and prep the vegetables the night before. In the morning, simply scramble the eggs, assemble, bake, and eat!

You may substitute $1^1/2$ cups shredded Cheddar cheese for the cheese sauce. SERVES 12

1. Prepare the sausage according to the package instructions. Drain.

2. Preheat the oven to 350°F.

3. In a large sauté pan, heat the oil. Add the garlic, scallions, black pepper, bell pepper, and olives, and sauté until the scallions are tender, 1 to 2 minutes. Add the sausage, and heat through.

4. In a medium sauté pan, scramble the eggs to your liking. Add the eggs to the vegetable-sausage mixture, and blend well. Mix in the blue cheese.

5. Place about $1/2$ cup of the egg mixture in the center of each tortilla. Fold in the ends and roll the tortillas into tight cylinders. Place the tortillas, seam side down, in a large baking pan. Ladle the cheese sauce over the tortillas, and cover with foil. Bake for 35 minutes, or until hot. Serve immediately.

Start the Day the Johnsonville Way

South of the Border
BREAKFAST TORTILLAS

This recipe may be prepared ahead of time and is easily doubled, so it's a great choice for larger groups. SERVES 6

10 Johnsonville Original
   Bratwurst Links, casings
   removed
1 tablespoon olive oil
1 tablespoon chopped garlic
$3/4$ cup diced onion
$3/4$ cup diced red bell
   pepper
$1/3$ cup sliced black olives
12 large eggs
$1^1/2$ cups shredded Monterey
   Jack cheese
28 ounces picante sauce
Twelve 12-inch tortillas

1. In a large skillet, cook and crumble the sausage over medium heat until browned, 8 to 10 minutes. Drain, and then place in a large bowl.

2. In a medium sauté pan, heat the oil. Add the garlic, onion, pepper, and olives, and sauté until the onion is tender, 1 to 2 minutes. Add this mixture to the bratwurst, reserving the pan.

3. In the same pan in which you sautéed the vegetables, scramble the eggs to your desired doneness. Add the eggs to the vegetable-bratwurst mixture.

4. Preheat the oven to 350°F.

5. In a medium bowl, blend 1 cup of the cheese and 1 cup of the picante sauce. Add to the egg mixture. Place about $1/2$ cup of this mixture in the center of each tortilla. Fold in the ends and roll the tortillas into tight cylinders. Place the tortillas, seam side down, in a pan large enough to hold twelve stuffed tortillas. Place the remaining picante sauce over the tortillas, and sprinkle with the remaining cheese. Cover with foil, and bake for 35 minutes, or until hot. Serve immediately.

Brats on the grill are a crowd-pleasing favorite at the local county fair!

BROWN SUGAR & HONEY
Breakfast Wraps

We in the Johnsonville kitchens love to blend sweet and savory flavors for breakfast. Here we're combining sweet apple butter and Brown Sugar & Honey Links with savory black olives, red onion, and Swiss cheese. The result? A simple and delicious dish that will keep your family coming back for more.

You may wish to substitute 2 tablespoons raspberry preserves blended with 2 tablespoons cream cheese for the apple butter. SERVES 4

12 Johnsonville Brown Sugar & Honey Links
8 large eggs, lightly beaten
$1/4$ cup sliced black olives
$1/4$ cup diced red onion, sautéed
$1/2$ cup shredded Swiss cheese
Salt
Freshly ground black pepper
Four 12-inch flour tortillas
$1/4$ cup apple butter

1. Prepare the links according to the package instructions. Drain.

2. In a medium nonstick sauté pan over low heat, scramble the eggs, olives, onion, cheese, salt, and pepper to your desired doneness.

3. Heat the flour tortillas according to the package instructions. Spread the apple butter on one side of each tortilla. Divide the egg mixture evenly among the tortillas, and line up three links beside each egg portion. Roll jellyroll-style and serve immediately.

Fruit and Nut Compote Wraps
WITH BROWN SUGAR & HONEY SAUSAGE

In this delectable recipe, mouth-watering Johnsonville Brown Sugar & Honey Links are paired with sweet and tart fruits. It's sure to become a family favorite.

If you can't find pomegranate seeds, substitute the fresh berries of your choice. Blueberries add color and a juicy pop. SERVES 4

One 20-ounce package
 Johnsonville Brown Sugar
 & Honey Links
1 tablespoon unsalted butter
1 banana, sliced
2 Granny Smith apples,
 peeled, cored, and diced
1 cup diced pineapple
$1^{1}/_{2}$ cups sliced green grapes
$^{1}/_{4}$ cup Calvados or other
 apple liqueur
4 tablespoons raspberry
 preserves
1 tablespoon cinnamon
$^{1}/_{2}$ cup pomegranate seeds
$^{1}/_{2}$ cup pecans, toasted
Eight 12-inch flour tortillas

1. Prepare the links according to the package instructions. Drain and set aside.

2. Melt the butter in a large sauté pan over medium heat. Add the banana, apples, pineapple, and grapes, and sauté for 2 minutes. Carefully add the apple liqueur, raspberry preserves, and $1^{1}/_{2}$ teaspoons of the cinnamon. Blend well. Stir in $^{1}/_{4}$ cup of the pomegranate seeds and $^{1}/_{4}$ cup of the pecans. Remove from heat.

3. Warm the tortillas according to the package instructions. Sprinkle one side of each tortilla with the remaining cinnamon. Spread one-eighth of the filling mixture down the center of each tortilla. Place three sausage links alongside the filling and roll. Place two stuffed tortillas, seam side down, on each serving plate, and top with the remaining pomegranate seeds and pecans.

— WAKE-UP *Frittata* —

The frittata is the omelet's Italian cousin. Instead of being folded inside as in an omelet, the ingredients in a frittata are mixed in with the eggs and cooked slowly over low heat. It's therefore round in shape and firmer than its French counterpart. If you like your cheese golden and bubbly, finish this delectable dish under the broiler.

Want to make the preparation even easier? Substitute frozen, presliced peppers and onions for the fresh. SERVES 8

One 12-ounce package Johnsonville Original Breakfast Patties
1 tablespoon minced garlic
$1/2$ red bell pepper, cut lengthwise into strips
$1/2$ yellow bell pepper, cut lengthwise into strips
$1/2$ green bell pepper, cut lengthwise into strips
$1/2$ cup sliced scallions, white and green parts
$1/2$ cup sliced black olives
8 large eggs
$1/2$ cup milk
Salt
Freshly ground black pepper
$1/2$ cup shredded Monterey Jack cheese
1 small Roma tomato, sliced

1. In a large skillet, cook and crumble the patties over medium heat until browned, about 5 minutes. Remove the sausage from the skillet, reserving the pan and all the drippings.

2. Add the garlic, red bell pepper, yellow bell pepper, green bell pepper, and scallions to the same skillet in which you browned the sausage. Sauté over medium heat until tender, about 3 minutes. Add the sausage and olives and heat through.

3. In a medium bowl, whisk together the eggs and milk. Season with salt and pepper. Pour the egg mixture over the sausage-vegetable mixture. Cover, and cook over low heat for 6 to 8 minutes, until the center is set.

4. Turn off the heat and remove the cover. Top with the cheese and tomato. Replace the lid and let stand 2 to 3 minutes, or until the cheese is melted. Cut into wedges and serve hot.

AUG.
1ST.

TONITE
Ralph Marterie
AND ORCHESTRA
8 P.M.
SHEBOYGAN ARMORY
BUTTONS 1¢

14,000 of BRATWURST DAY
PROFITS ARE GOING TO
DEVELOPEMENT OF QUARRY

Crowds line the street for the annual Brat Day Parade. The tradition continues today, though instead of a larger-than-life sausage float, the Big Taste Grill attracts the audience.

Proper Patty Care

Treat your Johnsonville Breakfast Patties right, and in return they'll cook up flavorful and juicy. Make up a nice place for them in the fridge, and they'll even stick around for 2 or 3 days.

Thaw Johnsonville Breakfast Patties thoroughly before cooking. You may use your microwave for this.

Cook them in a preheated skillet over medium-low heat for 8 to 10 minutes, turning them often. Sausage is cooked thoroughly when it reaches an internal temperature of 180°F.

Refrigerate cooked patties covered or in a closed container for a few days.

Reheat them in a microwave on high power for 1 to 2 minutes. Pan-heat them over medium heat for 3 to 5 minutes.

—— SUNRISE *Breakfast* CASSEROLE ——

This is one of our most popular breakfast recipes, and for good reason. Sunrise Breakfast Casserole is assembled the night before and refrigerated, allowing the flavors to infuse and you to sleep in a bit later. If you're serving a smaller group, no problem. Simply reduce the recipe or refrigerate the leftovers. It reheats wonderfully.

SERVES 12 TO 14

One 20-ounce package
   Johnsonville Original
   Breakfast Sausage Links
9 large eggs
3 cups milk
$1^1/_2$ teaspoons mustard
   powder
1 teaspoon salt
8 cups refrigerated or
   thawed frozen hash-brown
   potatoes
$1^1/_2$ cups shredded Cheddar
   cheese

1. Preheat the oven to 350°F.

2. Place the links in a baking dish. Bake for 15 to 20 minutes, turning once, until they are no longer pink. Drain and slice into $^1/_4$-inch coins.

3. In a large bowl, whisk together the eggs, milk, mustard, and salt. Add the potatoes, cheese, and sausage, and mix well to combine. Pour into a greased 13-by-9-by-2-inch baking dish. Cover, and refrigerate overnight. Remove the casserole from the refrigerator 30 minutes before baking.

4. Preheat the oven to 375°F. Bake for 1 hour, or until set and lightly golden brown. Let stand 10 minutes before cutting and serving.

Start the Day the Johnsonville Way

Sausage and Mushroom QUICHE

Another tasty Johnsonville breakfast that can be assembled the night before, Sausage and Mushroom Quiche can also be prepared as a "bottomless quiche" by eliminating the pastry crust.

You may substitute Johnsonville Original Bratwurst Links for the Johnsonville Original Breakfast Patties. SERVES 6 TO 8

One 12-ounce package Johnsonville Original Breakfast Patties

1 1/2 cups (8 ounces) sliced fresh mushrooms

1/4 cup finely chopped onion

1/4 cup finely chopped red bell pepper

1/4 cup finely chopped green bell pepper

One 3-ounce package cream cheese, softened

4 large eggs, lightly beaten

1/3 cup half-and-half

1 cup shredded Monterey Jack cheese

1 cup shredded Cheddar cheese

1/4 teaspoon salt

1/4 teaspoon freshly ground black pepper

Ground nutmeg

One 9-inch pastry shell, baked

1. Preheat the oven to 350°F.

2. In a large skillet, cook and crumble the sausage over medium-high heat for 3 minutes. Add the mushrooms, onion, red bell pepper, and green bell pepper. Cook, stirring frequently, until the sausage is no longer pink and the vegetables are tender, about 5 minutes. Drain.

3. In a large bowl, beat the cream cheese with a rubber spatula until smooth. Gradually beat in the eggs and half-and-half. Stir in the Monterey Jack cheese, Cheddar cheese, salt, pepper, and nutmeg to taste. Add the sausage mixture. Blend well.

4. Pour the mixture into the baked pastry shell. Bake for 40 to 45 minutes, until a knife inserted near the center comes out clean. If the edges of the pastry shell become too dark during cooking, you may need to cover with foil. Let stand 10 minutes before serving.

Sausage and Egg
TURNOVERS

This is a perfect breakfast for families on the go. Sausage and Egg Turnovers also make a great after-school snack. SERVES 8

8 Johnsonville Original
   Breakfast Patties
4 eggs, lightly beaten
1 tablespoon milk
$1/4$ teaspoon mustard
   powder
$1/4$ teaspoon salt
$1/8$ teaspoon freshly ground
   black pepper
1 teaspoon unsalted butter
One 16.3-ounce package
   large refrigerated flaky
   biscuits
$2^1/2$ tablespoons Thousand
   Island salad dressing
4 slices processed American
   cheese, halved

1. Preheat the oven to 350°F.

2. In a large covered skillet, cook the patties over medium heat, turning occasionally, until browned and a meat thermometer inserted in the center of the patties reads 180°F. Remove from the skillet and keep warm.

3. Combine the eggs, milk, mustard, salt, and pepper. Melt the butter in a large skillet over medium heat. Add the egg mixture. Cook, stirring frequently, until the eggs are set.

4. Separate the biscuit dough. On a lightly floured surface, roll out each biscuit into a circle that is 6 inches in diameter. On one-half of the circle, spread the dressing to within $1/2$ inch of the edge. Place a patty, 2 tablespoons of the egg mixture, and a cheese-slice half over the dressing. Fold the dough over; seal the edges with a fork. Place on an ungreased baking sheet. Bake for 14 to 17 minutes, until golden brown. Cool slightly before serving.

Slice and Dice, Cook and Crumble Like a Grillmeister

You'll see several knife cuts referenced throughout this book. Below, a guide to our favorites:

Bias Cut
To bias-slice sausage means to cut it at an angle. This exposes more surface to the flavorings and other ingredients and makes for a nicer presentation.

Half-Moon Cut
To make a half-moon cut, slice the sausage in half lengthwise, and then cut each half into slices.

Coin Slice
To coin-slice sausage, simply slice into rounds resembling coins.

Hinge-Cut/Slice
Hinge-cutting means cutting the sausage in half lengthwise, being careful not to cut it all the way through, then folding the sausage open but keeping it connected—like a door on its hinges. We also hinge-cut our buns from time to time.

Cook and Crumble
To cook and crumble sausage, remove it from its casings and brown it in a pan while breaking it into small pieces with a spatula or spoon, as you would ground beef.

Sauté
Sautéing means to cook or brown in a small amount of fat. Don't forget to stir.

For more sausage slicing techniques, see "Oops! Your Sausage Is Showing!" on page 172.

CAJUN "*By You*" BREAKFAST

In this bayou-inspired dish, corn bread biscuits are topped with per-fectly seasoned Johnsonville Hot 'n Spicy Bratwurst, and then slathered with a Cajun sauce. It's breakfast with a kick. SERVES 8

1 tablespoon olive oil

$1/2$ teaspoon minced garlic

$1/4$ cup diced onion

$1/4$ cup diced celery

$1/4$ cup diced red bell pepper

$1/4$ cup diced green bell pepper

$1/2$ teaspoon dried basil

$1/4$ teaspoon red pepper flakes

$1/4$ teaspoon white pepper

2 cups marinara sauce

Two 8.5-ounce packages corn bread mix

1 tablespoon Creole seasoning

4 Johnsonville Hot 'n Spicy Bratwurst

8 large eggs

10 ounces Monterey Jack cheese, shredded

1. To make the sauce: Heat the oil in a large pot over medium heat. Add the garlic, and sauté for 30 seconds.

2. Add the onion, celery, and red and green bell peppers. Cook until tender-crisp, about 5 min-utes. Add the basil, pepper flakes, and white pepper, and cook for 1 additional minute. Add the marinara sauce. Simmer for 10 minutes.

3. To make the dish: Prepare the corn bread according to the package instructions, using a 9-by-13-inch baking pan. Sprinkle with Creole seasoning and bake as directed. Cool completely.

4. Remove the bratwurst from the casings. Form each link into two sausage patties. Cook in a medium skillet over high heat until cooked through, about 1 minute each side. Keep warm.

5. Poach the eggs to your preference.

6. Using a knife or a biscuit cutter, cut the corn bread into eight equal portions. Place one sausage patty on each piece of corn bread. Cover with an egg. Top with the sauce and the cheese. Serve immediately.

Start the Day the Johnsonville Way

The 1959 Brat Days captured the spirit of community and creativity with a friendly boxcar race.

JOHNSONVILLE *Breakfast* EMPANADAS

Empanadas are small, savory pies that are eaten throughout Spain and in parts of South America. Like traditional empanadas, Johnsonville Breakfast Empanadas can be served warm or at room temperature. They are equally delicious for lunch or dinner. If you can't find taco cheese, make your own by combining shredded Monterey Jack and Cheddar cheeses. SERVES 8

One 16-ounce package
   Johnsonville Ground
   Sausage
5 large eggs
$1/2$ cup milk
$1^1/2$ teaspoons red pepper
   flakes
1 cup sliced scallions, white
   and green parts
1 cup diced tomato
Four 9-inch pastry shells
2 cups shredded taco cheese

1. Preheat the oven to 350°F.

2. In a large skillet, cook and crumble the sausage over high heat until browned, 3 to 5 minutes. Drain and set aside, reserving the skillet.

3. Whisk together the eggs, milk, pepper flakes, scallions, and tomato. Bring the same skillet in which you browned the sausage up to medium heat. Pour the egg mixture into the skillet, and cook until creamy and slightly loose, 2 to 3 minutes.

4. Place $3/4$ cup of the egg mixture on one-half of each pastry shell, leaving a $1/2$-inch border along the edge. Top with $1/2$ cup of the cheese and $1/2$ cup of the sausage. Fold the other half of the crust over the mixture to form a half-circle. Crimp the edges with a fork to seal.

5. With a sharp knife, pierce the empanadas to create steam vents. Place the pies on a lightly greased cookie sheet, and bake for 30 minutes, or until lightly golden. Allow to cool slightly, preferably on a cooling rack, and then cut each empanada in half to serve.

Apple Sausage Pancakes, page 4

South of the Border Breakfast Tortillas, page 18

Johnsonville Breakfast Empanadas, page 32

Hearty Minestrone, page 66

Sweet Sugar Piglets in Honey Blankets, page 33

Garlic-and-Sausage-Stuffed Mushrooms, page 36

Hot and Spicy New Orleans–Style Jambalaya, page 70

Fall Harvest Stew, page 73

—— SWEET SUGAR *piglets* IN HONEY BLANKETS —

This little piggy goes to market, this little piggy stays home and gets enveloped in a flaky, honey-coated blanket of goodness. It's a great recipe for kids of all ages. MAKES 14 BLANKETS

Two 8-ounce cylinders refrigerated croissant-roll dough
One 12-ounce package Johnsonville Brown Sugar & Honey Links, baked or pan-fried (follow the package instructions)
$1/2$ cup honey
2 tablespoons sugar
$1/2$ teaspoon cinnamon

1. Unroll the dough, and separate the sheets where perforated. Place a sausage on each triangle, and roll according to the package instructions.

2. With a pastry brush, spread the honey on top of the croissants. In a small bowl, mix the sugar and cinnamon together. Sprinkle the sugar-cinnamon mixture evenly over the honey. Bake according to the croissant package instructions. Serve immediately.

GET the *Party* STARTED!

GARLIC-AND-SAUSAGE-STUFFED MUSHROOMS

SAUSAGE APPETIZER LOAVES

PIZZA PARTY SNACKS

SAUSAGE CUPS

SAUSAGE STARS

SOUTHWEST PARTY DIP

ITALIAN CHEESE DIP

BRUSCHETTA WITH ITALIAN GROUND SAUSAGE,
OLIVES, AND CHEESE

JOHNSONVILLE ANTIPASTO

HOT AND SPICY STUFFED BANANA PEPPERS

TWO-BITE BRAT SANDWICHES

SAUCY WIENERS

PUFF PASTRY SAUSAGE TURNOVERS

CRUNCHY CORN BREAD AND CHEESY
CHEDDAR ROLL-UPS

*The brat-eating competition
of 1955. Fifty years later the
competition continues.*

Garlic-and-Sausage-Stuffed MUSHROOMS

These lovely stuffed mushroom caps are perfect for parties, with their savory flavor-packed punch and no-mess presentation. They're equally delicious fresh out of the oven or at room temperature.

MAKES 48 MUSHROOMS

One 19.76-ounce package Johnsonville Mild Italian Links, casings removed, or Italian Ground Sausage

8 ounces cream cheese, softened

3 garlic cloves, minced

2 tablespoons chopped fresh parsley

1 tablespoon lemon juice

$1/8$ teaspoon freshly ground black pepper, plus more for seasoning

48 large fresh button mushroom caps

Olive oil

Salt

4 ounces freshly grated Parmesan cheese

1. Preheat the oven to 450°F.

2. In a large skillet, cook and crumble the sausage over medium-high heat until browned, about 10 minutes. Drain.

3. In a food processor or blender, combine the cream cheese, garlic, parsley, lemon juice, and $1/8$ teaspoon pepper; mix until smooth.

4. Brush the mushroom caps with the oil. Place the caps, rounded side down, on a lightly greased baking sheet. Season to taste with salt and pepper.

5. Fill the mushroom caps with the sausage. Top each with $1/2$ teaspoon of the cream cheese mixture; sprinkle with the Parmesan cheese. Bake for 8 to 10 minutes, until lightly browned.

— SAUSAGE *Appetizer* LOAVES —

Think there's nothing better than a fresh-baked loaf of bread? Try these loaves, which are topped with creamy provolone and perfectly seasoned Johnsonville sausage crumbles, then baked up golden and delicious. Slices of this bread are wonderful on their own or served with a side of olive oil or chili oil. To make your own chili oil, add red pepper flakes or a whole chile pepper or two to olive oil and allow it to infuse at room temperature for at least 24 hours. Extra oil can be used to spice up salads.

MAKES THREE 10-INCH LOAVES

One 12-ounce package Johnsonville Original Breakfast Patties
$1/2$ cup chopped onion
$1/4$ cup chopped red bell pepper
$1/4$ cup chopped green bell pepper
One 1-pound loaf frozen bread dough, thawed
6 thin slices provolone cheese
1 large egg, lightly beaten

1. Preheat the oven to 400°F.

2. In a medium skillet, cook and crumble the sausage over medium-high heat for 3 minutes. Add the onion and peppers. Cook, stirring frequently, until the sausage is no longer pink, 3 to 5 additional minutes. Drain.

3. Divide the dough into thirds. Roll each portion into a 10-by-5-inch rectangle. Place two slices of cheese on each rectangle. Spread the sausage mixture over the cheese slices, coming to within $1/2$ inch of the edges. Roll jellyroll-style, starting with a long side.

4. Using some of the egg, seal the seam. Place the loaves, seam side down, on a greased baking sheet. Cut six shallow diagonal slits in the top of each loaf; brush with the remaining egg. Bake for 15 to 20 minutes, until golden brown. Let stand 10 minutes before slicing.

Get the Party Started!

Using just the right amount of heat, flavor, and TLC to get the job done, bratmeisters of 1956 demonstrate what's needed to create the perfect brat.

—— PIZZA *party* SNACKS ——————————

Great for during the game or at a kids' birthday party, Pizza Party Snacks take just 30 minutes to make. You may also use Johnsonville Italian Ground Sausage for this recipe. SERVES 8 TO 10

One 19.76-ounce package Johnsonville Mild Italian Links, casings removed, or one 16-ounce package Italian Ground Sausage

One 15^1/$_2$-ounce jar pizza sauce

1 loaf French bread, sliced in half lengthwise

One 8-ounce package shredded mozzarella cheese

1. Preheat the oven to 375°F.

2. In a large skillet, cook and crumble the sausage over medium heat until browned, 8 to 10 minutes. Drain, but do not remove the sausage from the skillet. Add the pizza sauce, and bring the mixture to a simmer over medium heat, about 5 minutes.

3. Spread the sausage-sauce mixture on both bread halves. Top with the cheese. Place on a baking sheet, and bake for 10 to 12 minutes, until the cheese is bubbly and lightly golden. Slice at an angle into 1-inch-wide pieces and serve.

Get the Party Started!

Sausage Cups

Don't let the frilly wonton wrapper cups fool you; these appetizers pack a lot of punch. Don't have a mini-muffin tin? Cut the wonton wrappers in half instead of quarters, and use a standard-size tin.

MAKES 4 TO 5 DOZEN

One 16-ounce package Johnsonville Mild Italian Ground Sausage
One 10-ounce package wonton wrappers
Two 8-ounce packages cream cheese, softened
1 tablespoon minced jalapeño pepper
1 tablespoon finely chopped fresh cilantro
$1/2$ tablespoon chili seasoning
2 cups shredded taco cheese, or a blend of Monterey Jack and Cheddar cheeses

1. Prepare the sausage according to the package instructions. Drain and dice.

2. Preheat the oven to 350°F.

3. Cut the wonton wrappers into fourths. Lightly grease a mini-muffin tin and press one wrapper into each cup. Bake for 3 minutes. Remove from the oven, but leave in the pan.

4. In a medium bowl, mix the cream cheese, jalapeño, cilantro, and seasoning. Fill the wonton cups with the sausage. Top with the cream cheese mixture. Sprinkle with the taco cheese, and bake until the cheese is bubbly and lightly golden, about 10 minutes. Serve warm.

Sausage Stars

Sausage Stars are sure to shine brightly at your next gathering. If you don't have a mini-muffin tin, cut the wonton wrappers in half instead of quarters and use a standard-size tin. MAKES 4 TO 5 DOZEN

Two 19.76-ounce packages
  Johnsonville Original
  Bratwurst Links, casings
  removed
2 cups shredded sharp
  Cheddar cheese
2 cups shredded Monterey
  Jack cheese
1 cup ranch salad dressing
1 cup sliced black olives
1 red bell pepper, chopped
One 10-ounce package
  wonton wrappers
Vegetable oil

1. Preheat the oven to 350°F.

2. In a large skillet, cook and crumble the sausage over medium heat until browned, 8 to 10 minutes. Drain.

3. In a large bowl, combine the sausage, Cheddar cheese, Monterey Jack cheese, dressing, olives, and pepper.

4. Cut the wonton wrappers into fourths. Lightly grease a mini-muffin tin, and press one wrapper into each cup. Brush with the oil, and bake for 7 minutes, or until golden. Remove the cups from the tin, and place them on a baking sheet.

5. Fill each muffin cup with the sausage mixture. Bake for 7 minutes, or until the cheese is bubbly and golden. Serve warm.

SOUTHWEST *party* DIP

Our slightly sweet Mild Cooked Italian Sausage packs plenty of authentic Italian flavor into a convenient precooked link. We suggest keeping a pack or two on hand for impromptu parties, where they can be used in this festive dip or served with cheese and crackers. SERVES 10

One 16-ounce can refried beans
2 tablespoons sliced jalapeño peppers
Two 4-ounce cans green chiles, drained and chopped
One 16-ounce package Johnsonville Mild Cooked Italian Sausage, coin-sliced
$1^1/_2$ cups shredded mild Cheddar cheese
$1^1/_2$ cups shredded Monterey Jack cheese
1 cup mild thick-and-chunky salsa
Tortilla chips

1. Preheat the oven to 350°F.

2. Combine the beans, peppers, chiles, and sausage in a large bowl. Spread the mixture evenly on the bottom of a 9-by-13-inch glass dish. Top with the Cheddar and Monterey Jack cheeses. Bake for 20 to 25 minutes, until the cheese is bubbly and golden.

3. Top with the salsa, and serve warm with the tortilla chips.

ITALIAN *Cheese* DIP

This is our spin on the traditional Velveeta cheese dip. We've added a delicate blend of seasonings, plus the irresistible flavor of our Mild Italian Links. This ooey-gooey dip is also great served over steak, mashed potatoes, or nachos. You may also use Johnsonville Italian Ground Sausage for this recipe. SERVES 8

One 19.76-ounce package Johnsonville Mild Italian Links, casings removed, or Italian Ground Sausage

One 32-ounce package Velveeta cheese, cubed

One 16-ounce jar thick and chunky salsa

1 tablespoon ground fennel seed

3 garlic cloves, minced

1 teaspoon ground aniseed

1/4 teaspoon dried basil

1 round loaf bread

1. In a large skillet, cook and crumble the sausage over medium heat until browned, 8 to 10 minutes. Drain.

2. Place the cheese in a large microwave-safe bowl, and microwave on high, stirring every 2 minutes, until melted. Add the salsa, fennel, garlic, anise, basil, and sausage. Microwave on high until hot.

3. Hollow the center of the bread, and use it as the serving dish for the dip.

BRUSCHETTA WITH
Italian Ground Sausage,
OLIVES, AND CHEESE

Bruschetta is an Italian specialty of grilled or toasted bread slices topped with a savory garnish such as tomatoes and basil, puréed cannellini beans, or anchovies. It originated as a method of testing the season's olive oil harvest, but in this case it's just another simple and delicious preparation that shows off our ground sausage's authentic Italian flavor.

Use the Italian bread of your choice. Rustic, open-textured breads such as ciabatta work best. SERVES 8 TO 10

One 16-ounce package Johnsonville Mild Italian Ground Sausage
1 loaf Italian bread
$1/2$ cup olive oil
One 7-ounce jar roasted red peppers
7 ounces black olives, sliced
$1/2$ pound thinly sliced provolone cheese

1. Heat the grill.

2. In a large skillet, cook and crumble the sausage over medium heat until browned, 8 to 10 minutes. Drain.

3. Slice the bread into $3/4$-inch slices, and brush the tops and bottoms with the oil. Grill until golden on one side. Flip, and grill the other side. Remove from the grill, and cover with the sausage, peppers, olives, and cheese. Place on a large sheet of foil and seal loosely, making certain the foil does not touch the cheese; place on the grill. Cover, and cook for 5 minutes, or until the cheese is melted and the bruschetta is warm.

—— JOHNSONVILLE *Antipasto* ——————

An antipasto is a hot or cold hors d'oeuvre that tantalizes the taste buds and dazzles the eye. Bring this blend of perfectly seasoned, pre-cooked Garlic Summer Sausage, colorful vegetables, sharp Cheddar cheese, and tangy Italian dressing to your next potluck, and let the good times roll! SERVES 6 TO 8

10 ounces cherry tomatoes

3 cups Johnsonville Garlic Summer Sausage, cut into $1/4$-inch cubes

6 ounces large black olives, left whole

$1/2$ cup chopped red onion

4 cups fresh broccoli florets

4 cups fresh cauliflower florets

3 cups sliced carrots

12 ounces fresh button mushrooms

One 8-ounce jar sweet-and-sour cocktail onions

1 bunch scallions, white and light-green parts, chopped

3 cups cubed sharp Cheddar cheese

Two 12-ounce bottles Italian dressing

Place all ingredients in a large bowl, and mix well to combine. Serve at room temperature or chilled.

Stuffed Banana Peppers

*Banana peppers are long yellow sweet peppers that are mild and there-
fore excellent for stuffing. Yellow wax peppers are spicier and often
mistaken for banana peppers, so unless you'd
like your socks knocked off—which we do
like from time to time round Johnsonville—
shop carefully.* SERVES 8

One 19.76-ounce package
  Johnsonville Hot 'n Spicy
  Bratwurst
8 banana peppers
One 8-ounce package cream
  cheese
$^1/_2$ cup diced scallions, white
  and green parts
$^3/_4$ cup shredded taco
  cheese
$^3/_4$ cup shredded Monterey
  Jack cheese

1. Remove the bratwurst from the casings. In a
large skillet, cook and crumble the sausage over
high heat until browned, 15 to 20 minutes.

2. To roast the peppers: If you have a gas range,
char the peppers over an open flame by placing
them directly on the burners. When the skin becomes blackened and blistered, turn the peppers
so that each side becomes completely charred.
Allow the peppers to cool slightly, then rinse the
skins off under cool running water and pat dry.
Cut the peppers in half lengthwise and scoop
out the seeds. You could also use the above
method on a grill. If you have an electric range,
place the whole peppers in a shallow baking dish
and drizzle them with olive oil. Cover the pan
with aluminum foil, and bake until the skin blis-
ters, 30 to 45 minutes. Immediately place the
peppers into a large resealable plastic bag and
seal, being careful not to burn yourself. Allow
the peppers to steam inside the bag until they

are cool enough to handle. Remove them from the bag, and rub the skins off under cool running water. Pat dry. You may wish to save the oil that remains in the baking dish to use on salads. Cut the peppers in half lengthwise and scoop out the seeds.

3. Preheat the broiler.

4. Place the browned bratwurst, the cream cheese, scallions, taco cheese, and Monterey Jack cheese in a large mixing bowl. Mix well to combine.

5. Spoon the mixture into the pepper halves, and broil for 3 to 4 minutes, until the cheese is melted and the mixture is hot. Serve immediately.

Where Is Charlie Murphy?

He first graced our television screens in 1981: Charlie Murphy, the unfortunate soul who minded his own business while grilling plump, juicy Johnsonville brats at the end of his pier until spied by a pesky neighbor. When asked what he was grilling, Charlie panicked.

"Ah . . . nothing," he replied, quickly trying to stand in front of the grill to hide his brats.

"Come on, I know a Johnsonville brat when I see one," the neighbor said.

"They're *not* Johnsonville," Charlie lied.

The neighbor moved the grill mitt that Charlie had used to hide his treasured sausage. "They *are* Johnsonville! I love 'em!"

Quickly realizing the terrible mistake he'd made, Charlie begged the neighbor to come back tomorrow.

But it was too late. The neighbor had already cupped his hands around his mouth and begun yelling, "Charlie Murphy's cooking Johnsonville brats!" The words "Johnsonville brats" echoed across the lake several times, bringing with them dozens of party crashers: campers, boaters, anyone else within earshot. As Charlie so famously said at the commercial's close, "When you're good, word gets around fast."

Those of you who reenact this scene every time you grill Johnsonville brats—yes, you—may wonder whatever became of the elusive Charlie Murphy. Some say that he retreated to his Northwoods Wisconsin cabin, others that he's living a life of anonymity in downtown Chicago. We're not sure, but we'd like to think that, wherever he is, Charlie Murphy's grilling Johnsonville brats.

Johnsonville® Fresh Sausage – 30 second TV

VIDEO: We open on a shot of a lake dock, on a sunny, summer day.
AUDIO: Birds singing and waves rolling.

VIDEO: Close up of steaming brats on the grill.
AUDIO: Brats sizzling.

VIDEO: The neighbor sneaks up behind Charlie and taps him on the shoulder.
CHARLIE: (suprised) "Aaahh......"
NEIGHBOR: "Hi Charlie."

CHARLIE: "ha...you..ah..you startled me."
NEIGHBOR: "Whatcha cooking?"
CHARLIE: "Ah...nothing."

VIDEO: Charlie tries to stand in front of his grill to hide the brats.
NEIGHBOR: "Come on, I know a Johnsonville Brat when I see one."
CHARLIE: "They're *not* Johnsonville."

VIDEO: The neighbor uncovers the packaged brats near Charlie's grill.
NEIGHBOR: "They *are* Johnsonville! I love 'em!"

CHARLIE: "Could you come back tomorrow please?"
VIDEO: Neighbor turns to yell...
CHARLIE: "Oh please don't do that!"

NEIGHBOR: "Charlie Murphy's cooking Johnsonville Brats!"™ (echo)

VIDEO: Campers turn to look toward the call.
AUDIO: (echo)

VIDEO: Boaters turn to look toward the call.
AUDIO: (echo)

ANNCR: "Folks can't resist the simply great taste....."

ANNCR: "......of Johnsonville Brats."

A 1981 television commercial storyboard

—TWO-BITE *Brat* SANDWICHES—

Dare we say these sandwiches are cute? But don't judge a brat by its size. The sweet-and-sour flavor and husky aroma of Two-Bite Brats are anything but dainty. MAKES 24 MINI-SANDWICHES

48 Johnsonville Little
  Smokies
One 8-ounce jar coarse-
  ground mustard
24 small dinner rolls, hinge-
  sliced
2 small yellow onions, thinly
  sliced
24 slices dill pickle
Ketchup

1. Heat the Little Smokies and keep them warm.

2. Spread the mustard onto the bottom half of each roll. Add two Little Smokies per roll. Top with the onions, pickles, and ketchup. Serve warm.

Saucy Wieners

The name says it all. They're wieners, they're saucy, and they're perfect for your next party. SERVES 18 TO 24

12 ounces spicy brown
  mustard
1 pound brown sugar
Two 16-ounce packages
  Johnsonville Natural
  Casing Wieners, sliced into
  $^1/_2$-inch pieces

1. Heat the mustard and brown sugar in a large saucepan over medium heat until the sugar begins to caramelize, about 3 minutes. Add the wieners, and simmer for 7 additional minutes.

2. Keep warm, and serve on toothpicks.

PUFF PASTRY *Sausage* TURNOVERS

Any Johnsonville Breakfast Sausage Links are great in place of the Mild Cooked Italian Sausage in this recipe. Simply prepare the links according to the package instructions, dice them, and proceed with the recipe.

One 16-ounce package
  Johnsonville Mild Cooked
  Italian Sausage, diced
1$^1/_2$ cups shredded Cheddar
  cheese
$^3/_4$ cup ricotta cheese
$^1/_3$ cup sliced scallions, white
  and green parts
1 large egg, lightly beaten
One 17.25-ounce package
  frozen puff pastry, thawed

To give the turnovers a deeper-golden color, brush them with an egg wash just prior to baking. To make the egg wash, whisk 1 large egg with 1 tablespoon cool water.

Puff Pastry Sausage Turnovers are also a delight for breakfast. MAKES 50 TURNOVERS

1. Preheat the oven to 400°F.

2. Combine the sausage, Cheddar cheese, ricotta cheese, scallions, and egg in a large bowl.

3. On a lightly floured surface, roll each sheet of the puff pastry into a 12$^1/_2$-inch square. Cut each sheet into twenty-five equal squares.

4. Place 1 rounded teaspoonful of filling on each square. Fold the squares to form triangles; crimp the edges together with a fork.

5. Place the turnovers on a lightly greased baking sheet. Bake for 15 minutes, or until golden brown.

CRUNCHY CORN BREAD
and Cheesy Cheddar
ROLL-UPS

These are delicious and easy to handle at parties. You may also wish to try Crunchy Corn Bread and Cheesy Cheddar Roll-Ups for lunch. They're excellent with a cup of soup. MAKES 5 ROLL-UPS

1 cup cornmeal

2 teaspoons red pepper flakes

$^1/_2$ teaspoon minced garlic

1 teaspoon dried parsley

One 11$^1/_2$-ounce cylinder corn bread twist breadsticks

One 16-ounce package Johnsonville Beddar with Cheddar Smoked Sausage

1. Preheat the oven to 350°F.

2. In a medium bowl, combine the cornmeal, pepper flakes, garlic, and parsley.

3. Place two breadsticks end to end. Pinch them together to form one long breadstick. Press or roll each breadstick to form a 7-by-1$^1/_2$-inch strip. Wrap each breadstick around a link. Press the ends of the breadsticks around the ends of the links to seal. Dredge in the cornmeal mixture, pressing lightly to coat the roll-up.

4. Place on a baking sheet, and bake for 15 minutes, or until golden brown.

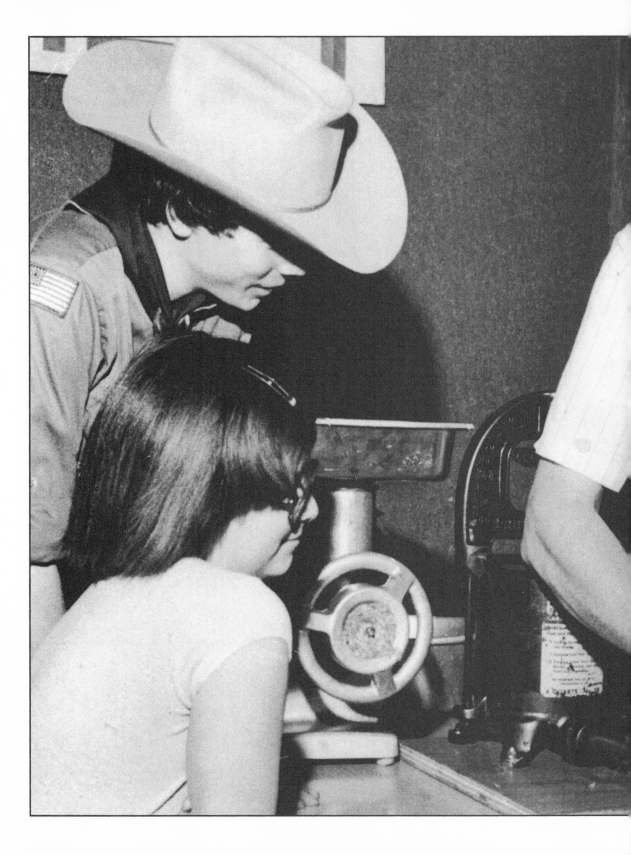

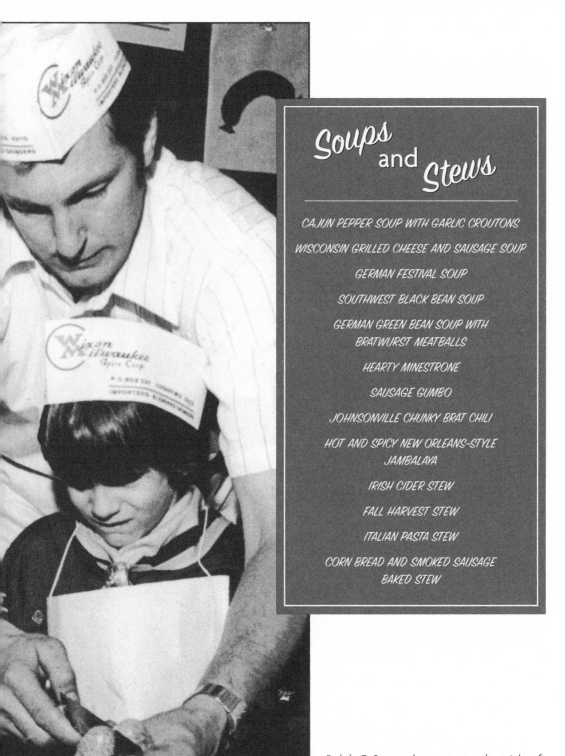

Soups and Stews

CAJUN PEPPER SOUP WITH GARLIC CROUTONS

WISCONSIN GRILLED CHEESE AND SAUSAGE SOUP

GERMAN FESTIVAL SOUP

SOUTHWEST BLACK BEAN SOUP

GERMAN GREEN BEAN SOUP WITH
BRATWURST MEATBALLS

HEARTY MINESTRONE

SAUSAGE GUMBO

JOHNSONVILLE CHUNKY BRAT CHILI

HOT AND SPICY NEW ORLEANS-STYLE
JAMBALAYA

IRISH CIDER STEW

FALL HARVEST STEW

ITALIAN PASTA STEW

CORN BREAD AND SMOKED SAUSAGE
BAKED STEW

Ralph C. Stayer demonstrates the tricks of the trade to his sons, Ralph III and Mike, during their visit with the local Boy Scout troop in 1978.

Cajun Pepper Soup
WITH GARLIC CROUTONS

If you like baked French onion soup, you'll love this zestier offering made with red, yellow, and green bell peppers. For a smoky flavor, you may substitute Johnsonville New Orleans Style Smoked Sausage for the Hot 'n Spicy Bratwurst. SERVES 8 TO 10

One 19.76-ounce package Johnsonville Hot 'n Spicy Bratwurst

2 tablespoons olive oil

1 red bell pepper, cut into strips

1 yellow bell pepper, cut into strips

1 green bell pepper, cut into strips

1 large yellow onion, cut into strips

Six 10^1/$_2$-ounce cans chicken broth

1 stick unsalted butter

1 tablespoon minced garlic

1 loaf French bread, cut into ^{1}/$_4$-inch-thick slices as croutons

Cajun seasoning

2^1/$_2$ cups shredded Monterey Jack cheese

1. Prepare the links according to the package instructions. Slice into ^{1}/$_4$-inch coins and set aside.

2. Place the oil in a large stockpot over medium heat. Add the peppers and onion. Sauté until tender, 4 to 5 minutes. Add the broth and the bratwurst coins. Bring to a simmer. Cook for 15 minutes.

3. Preheat the oven to 350°F.

4. Melt the butter in a large sauté pan over high heat. Add the garlic, and remove from heat. Let stand 5 minutes. Brush the croutons with the garlic butter. Sprinkle with the seasoning. Bake on a sheet pan for 5 to 6 minutes, until golden brown and crunchy.

5. Fill ovenproof bowls with soup. Place a crouton on each serving, and cover with ^{1}/$_4$ cup of the shredded cheese. Bake for 5 minutes, or until the cheese is bubbly and golden brown.

WISCONSIN *Grilled Cheese* AND SAUSAGE SOUP

Brats, beer, and cheese: the holy trinity of Wisconsin cuisine. What more do you need? SERVES 4

2 tablespoons unsalted
  butter
1/2 cup diced yellow onion
1/4 cup diced carrot
1/4 cup diced celery
1 teaspoon minced garlic
1/2 cup all-purpose flour
One 14 1/2-ounce can chicken
  broth, chilled
1/2 cup dark beer, chilled
2 cups shredded Cheddar
  cheese
1 teaspoon mustard powder
One 16-ounce package
  Johnsonville Smoked Brats,
  bias-sliced
Salt
Chopped fresh parsley for
  garnish

1. Melt the butter in a large skillet over medium heat. Add the onion, carrot, celery, and garlic. Sauté until the vegetables are softened, about 2 minutes. Add the flour, whisking constantly until all the liquid is absorbed.

2. Add the cold broth and beer, whisking constantly. Gradually add 1 cup of the cheese, stirring to aid in the melting process. Simmer for 5 minutes.

3. Add the mustard and sausage. Simmer until the flour taste is completely cooked out, 20 to 25 additional minutes. Season to taste with salt.

4. Pour the soup into ovenproof bowls. Sprinkle with the remaining cheese; place under the broiler until the cheese is bubbly and golden brown. Sprinkle with chopped parsley and serve.

— GERMAN *Festival* SOUP —

This rustic soup, a perfect accompaniment to any cold-weather meal, is also hearty enough to serve as a main course. SERVES 8 TO 12

One 19.76-ounce package
  Johnsonville Original
  Bratwurst Links
Eight 14^1/$_2$-ounce cans
  chicken broth
2 large rutabagas, peeled and
  cut into strips
2 turnips, peeled and
  coarsely chopped
1 butternut squash, peeled
  and coarsely chopped
1 medium yellow onion,
  coarsely chopped
2 medium Roma tomatoes,
  chopped
2 cups frozen French-style
  green beans
3 celery ribs, coarsely
  chopped
3 carrots, coarsely chopped
1^1/$_2$ cups fresh, frozen, or
  canned (drained) whole-
  kernel corn
^{1}/$_2$ head green cabbage,
  coarsely chopped
1^2/$_3$ cups quick-cooking
  barley
2 tablespoons minced garlic
Salt
Freshly ground black pepper

1. Prepare the links according to the package instructions. Slice into ^{1}/$_4$-inch coins.

2. Pour the broth into a large stockpot. Add the rutabagas, turnips, squash, and onion. Bring to a boil over high heat. Add the tomatoes, beans, celery, carrots, corn, cabbage, barley, and garlic. Season to taste with salt and pepper. Cover, and reduce heat to medium-low. Simmer for 25 to 30 minutes, until all the vegetables are tender.

3. Skim any impurities that may have risen to the soup's surface during the cooking process. Add the bratwurst and cook for a few minutes to heat through. Adjust seasoning if necessary.

—SOUTHWEST *Black Bean* SOUP—

This colorful soup is so complex in flavor that your family and friends will believe you spent hours making it. Your secret's safe with us.

For added color and flavor, garnish with coarsely chopped cilantro. SERVES 6 TO 8

Two 15-ounce cans low-
   sodium black beans,
   undrained
One 16-ounce package
   Johnsonville Smoked Brats,
   sliced
One 14^1/$_2$-ounce can diced
   tomatoes, undrained
3 garlic cloves, minced
2 teaspoons lime juice
^{1}/$_4$ teaspoon red pepper
   flakes
^{1}/$_3$ cup sour cream
^{1}/$_4$ cup diced yellow bell
   pepper

1. Bring the beans, brats, tomatoes, garlic, lime juice, and pepper flakes to a boil in a large stockpot over high heat. Reduce heat to medium-low, and simmer for 15 minutes.

2. Place the soup in individual serving bowls. Top with dollops of sour cream. Sprinkle with the diced pepper, and serve immediately.

Johnsonville Time Line:
A Legacy of Great-Tasting Sausage

What started as a mom-and-pop butcher shop has today become the number one sausage brand in America, with Johnsonville's BIG TASTE FROM A SMALL TOWN available in over forty countries.

1945
The BIG TASTE of Johnsonville is born. Ralph F. and Alice B. Stayer open a butcher shop and name it after their quaint hometown of Johnsonville, Wisconsin.

1950s
Johnsonville sausage is in such demand that the Stayers expand into nearby communities.

1965
Ralph C. Stayer, son of Ralph F. and Alice B. Stayer, returns from college and joins the family business.

1970s
Colorful Johnsonville trucks begin gracing state highways to deliver Johnsonville's BIG TASTE to stores throughout Wisconsin.

1978
Ralph C. Stayer becomes president of the company and launches widespread out-of-state expansion efforts. A second plant is built, and Johnsonville begins airing its popular TV commercials.

1984
Launa Stayer starts the company's first direct-sales force and continues to expand into new markets across the country. By the end of the 1980s, Johnsonville sausage is available in forty-seven states.

1995
Johnsonville Sausage celebrates its fiftieth anniversary by sponsoring a large outdoor event, free to the public at a local fairgrounds. To commemorate the anniversary, Johnsonville unveils the first Big Taste Grill, the world's largest touring grill.

2000
Johnsonville sausage is sold in thirty-three countries around the world and in all fifty states.

2004
Johnsonville sausage becomes the number one sausage brand in America.

2005
Johnsonville celebrates sixty years of sausage history by creating a third Big Taste Grill. The fleet now includes the Miss Alice, Miss Shelly, and Miss Launa Big Taste Grills. The three grills bring the BIG TASTE to more than a thousand sporting and special events per year.

2006
The first Johnsonville cookbook is published!

The Kraut Barrel Dunking Tank was a popular attraction during 1968's Brat Days.

KRAUT
BARREL

German Green Bean Soup

WITH BRATWURST MEATBALLS

*A hearty, German-inspired soup with meatballs made from our per-
fectly seasoned bratwurst, German Green Bean Soup with Bratwurst
Meatballs will make your children beg to eat their green vegetables!
If you don't have fresh green beans, use frozen.* SERVES 8 TO 10

MEATBALLS

One 19.76-ounce package
  Johnsonville Original
  Bratwurst Links, casings
  removed
1/3 cup bread crumbs
1 large egg
1/4 cup milk
2 garlic cloves, minced

SOUP

1 stick unsalted butter
1 1/2 pounds fresh green
  beans, trimmed and cut
  into 1-inch pieces
1/4 cup diced yellow onion
3 medium russet potatoes,
  peeled and coarsely
  chopped
1/2 cup all-purpose flour
2 cups cold milk
1 cup cold heavy cream
4 teaspoons chicken base
2 garlic cloves, minced
1 Turkish bay leaf
Salt
Freshly ground black pepper

1. To make the meatballs: Preheat the oven to
450°F.

2. In a large bowl, combine the bratwurst, bread
crumbs, egg, milk, and garlic. Let stand until all
the liquid is absorbed, about 2 minutes.

3. Using the palms of your hands, roll the mixture into meatballs the size of a nickel. Place on
an ungreased baking sheet, and bake for 10 minutes, or until no longer pink.

4. To make the soup: Melt the butter in a large
stockpot over medium-high heat. Add the beans,
onion, and potatoes, and sauté until the vegetables are softened and the butter is lightly
browned, 2 to 3 minutes.

5. Add the flour, whisking until all the liquid is
absorbed. Pour in the cold milk, cream, and 8
cups of cold water, whisking constantly. Adjust
heat to medium. Add the base, garlic, and bay
leaf. Season to taste with salt and pepper. Sim-

Local dignitaries announce the official opening of the Bratwurst Day festivities.

mer, stirring frequently, until the vegetables are tender and the flour taste is completely cooked out, 35 to 40 minutes.

6. Add the meatballs and cook for a few minutes to heat through; adjust seasoning if necessary. Remove the bay leaf before serving.

Hearty Minestrone

Traditional minestrone contains pasta, beans, or rice, but we're pretty sure if early Italians had Johnsonville Italian Links they'd have used them, too.

You may wish to serve Hearty Minestrone with a dollop of pesto and freshly grated Parmesan cheese on top. MAKES 3½ QUARTS

One 19.76-ounce package Johnsonville Mild or Sweet Italian Links
1 red bell pepper, chopped
1 medium yellow onion, chopped
1 cup chopped celery
Two 14½-ounce cans chicken broth
1 cup dry red wine
One 16-ounce can chopped tomatoes, undrained
One 15½-ounce can Great Northern beans, rinsed and drained
2 cups uncooked shell pasta
1 medium zucchini, chopped
1 medium russet potato, peeled and chopped
½ teaspoon chopped fresh oregano
½ teaspoon chopped fresh basil
Salt
Freshly ground black pepper

1. Remove the sausages from their casings and cut the meat into coarse chunks.

2. In a large stockpot, brown the sausage over medium heat until it is golden, 5 to 6 minutes. Add the bell pepper, onion, and celery; sauté for 5 to 6 minutes.

3. Add the broth, wine, tomatoes, beans, pasta, zucchini, potato, oregano, and basil. Bring to a boil. Season to taste with salt and pepper. Reduce heat to low, cover, and simmer for 20 to 25 minutes. Serve warm.

Sausage Gumbo

Gumbo is a robust Creole dish made with vegetables and spicy meat or shellfish. Though some gumbos begin with a dark roux, we use okra as a thickening agent. It gives our Sausage Gumbo a stewlike stick-to-your-ribs consistency. SERVES 6 TO 8

1/4 cup vegetable oil

1 large yellow onion, chopped

1 red bell pepper, chopped

1 celery rib, chopped

1/4 cup all-purpose flour

2 cans chicken broth, chilled

Two 16-ounce packages Johnsonville Smoked Brats, bias-sliced

1 1/2 cups sliced fresh okra

2 tablespoons Cajun seasoning

3 cups cooked long-grain rice, warm

1. Heat the oil in a large stockpot over medium heat. Add the onion, pepper, and celery, and sauté until the vegetables are softened, about 3 minutes. Add the flour, whisking until all the liquid is absorbed. Pour in the cold broth, whisking constantly. Bring to a boil.

2. Add the brats, okra, and seasoning, and cook until the vegetables are tender and the flour taste is completely cooked out, 15 to 20 minutes. Serve over the rice.

JOHNSONVILLE *Chunky Brat* CHILI

One of our most famous recipes, Johnsonville Chunky Brat Chili makes generous portions, and friends and family won't be able to get enough. If you're lucky enough to have any leftovers, it's even better reheated.

Serve with thick slices of bread: you'll want to sop up every drop of flavor. SERVES 10 TO 12

1 tablespoon olive oil

Two 19.76-ounce packages Johnsonville Original Bratwurst Links, coarsely chopped

3 tablespoons crushed garlic

7 tablespoons dark chili powder

2 tablespoons unsweetened cocoa powder

One 16-ounce bottle beer

One 28-ounce can whole stewed tomatoes, undrained

One 28-ounce can diced tomatoes, undrained

One 30-ounce can hot chili beans, undrained

One 15$1/4$-ounce can black beans, rinsed and drained

One 16-ounce can whole-kernel corn, drained

One 16-ounce can small whole onions, drained

3 cups coarsely chopped celery

2 cups coarsely chopped yellow onion

1 green bell pepper, roasted (see page 46) and coarsely chopped

1 red bell pepper, roasted (see page 46) and coarsely chopped

1 bunch scallions, white parts only, sliced

2 teaspoons cumin

1 tablespoon onion powder

$1/2$ teaspoon red pepper flakes

1 teaspoon freshly ground white pepper

1 teaspoon cayenne pepper

Juice and pulp of 1 lime

1 tablespoon sugar

5 tablespoons chopped fresh cilantro

Salt

Freshly ground black pepper

1. Heat the oil in a very large stockpot over medium-high heat. Add the bratwurst, 1 teaspoon of the garlic, 1 teaspoon of the chili powder, and the cocoa powder, and sauté until the sausage is browned, 6 to 8 minutes. Stir often to avoid burning. Drain.

2. Add the beer, stewed tomatoes, diced tomatoes, hot chili beans, black beans, corn, small whole onions, celery, chopped onion, bell peppers, scallions, cumin, onion powder, remaining garlic, pepper flakes, white pepper, and cayenne pepper. Reduce the heat to low, and simmer for 45 minutes.

3. Add the remaining chili powder, the lime juice and pulp, sugar, and cilantro. Cook an additional 15 minutes. Season to taste with salt and black pepper.

Six young men pedal their way down Main Street in a 1950s Brat Days parade.

Soups and Stews

New Orleans–Style
JAMBALAYA

You're probably familiar with jambalaya, which is a heavily seasoned Creole rice dish made with shrimp, oysters, ham, or chicken. Our New Orleans–Style Smoked Sausage is an andouille sausage that's already packed with authentic Creole seasonings and just a bit of bite. It's fantastic in this recipe, which is bound to become one of your favorites.

SERVES 10 TO 12

2/3 cup vegetable oil

2 yellow onions, diced

1 cup diced celery

2 red bell peppers, diced

2 green bell peppers, diced

1/2 tablespoon dried thyme

2 cups diced Roma tomatoes

4 garlic cloves, minced

16 ounces boneless, skinless chicken breast, cubed

8 to 10 links Johnsonville New Orleans–Style Smoked Sausage, sliced

1 teaspoon salt

12 drops Tabasco sauce

1 tablespoon Worcestershire sauce

1 teaspoon cayenne pepper

2 teaspoons Creole seasoning

3 cups uncooked long-grain rice

Four 10 1/2-ounce cans chicken broth

3 pounds shrimp, peeled and deveined

1. Heat the oil in a large saucepan over medium heat. Add the onions, celery, peppers, and thyme. Sauté until deep golden in color, 8 to 10 minutes.

2. Add the tomatoes and garlic, and sauté another 2 minutes. Stir in the chicken and sausage, and cook for an additional 10 minutes.

3. Stir in the salt, Tabasco sauce, Worcestershire sauce, cayenne pepper, Creole seasoning, and rice. Sauté, stirring constantly, for 3 minutes. Add the broth, and mix well.

4. Reduce the heat to low, and cook until the rice is tender and the liquid is almost gone, about 20 minutes. Add the shrimp; cover, and cook until the shrimp is pink and cooked through, about 2 minutes. Serve immediately.

Cider Stew

This sweet-and-sour stew is a unique accompaniment to the grilled Johnsonville sausage of your choice. It's also great served with rustic bread to mop up every bit of flavorful liquid. SERVES 8 TO 10

One 19.76-ounce package Johnsonville Original Bratwurst Links

8 ounces baby carrots

2 medium red-skinned potatoes, coarsely chopped

1 large yellow onion, coarsely chopped

2 Granny Smith apples, coarsely chopped

$1/4$ cup coarsely chopped green cabbage

2 quarts apple cider

3 tablespoons cider vinegar

$1/2$ cup chicken broth

2 tablespoons cornstarch

Salt

Freshly ground black pepper

1. Grill the links according to the package instructions, and coin-slice them.

2. Place the carrots, potatoes, onion, apples, cabbage, cider, vinegar, and broth in a large stockpot. Bring to a simmer over medium heat. Simmer for 30 minutes.

3. In a small bowl, whisk together the cornstarch with 2 tablespoons cold water to create a slurry. Stir into the soup.

4. Add the sliced bratwurst. Reduce heat, and simmer, stirring frequently, until the stew is thickened and the graininess of the slurry is cooked out, about 2 minutes. Season to taste with salt and pepper.

A grillmeister tempers his flames to ensure that his Johnsonville brats grill up plump and juicy.

—— FALL *Harvest* STEW ——————

Fall Harvest Stew is as colorful as the Wisconsin countryside that in-spired it. To capture the flavor of autumn fully, you may wish to add wild mushrooms. SERVES 6

10 Johnsonville bratwurst

Four 14^1/$_2$-ounce cans chicken broth

^{1}/$_4$ cup coarse-ground mustard

3 pounds red potatoes, cubed

1 pound carrots, peeled and coarsely chopped

3 yellow onions, sliced

1 celery rib, cut into 1-inch pieces

4 tomatoes, cut into wedges

Salt

Freshly ground black pepper

2 tablespoons cornstarch

1. Grill the bratwurst according to the package instructions, and slice into 1-inch pieces.

2. Place the broth and mustard in a large stock-pot. Add the remaining ingredients, except the cornstarch, making certain everything is covered with liquid. If not, add additional broth as needed. Cook over medium heat until the veg-etables are tender, about 20 minutes.

3. In a small bowl, whisk together the cornstarch and 2 tablespoons cold water to create a slurry. Stir the slurry into the stew, and cook 2 addi-tional minutes. Adjust the seasoning to taste with more salt and pepper. Serve hot.

ITALIAN *Pasta* STEW

This is a very simple but satisfying stew that takes little effort to prepare. Serve it with warm, crusty garlic bread. SERVES 6

1 tablespoon olive oil

1 large yellow onion, coarsely chopped

4 red-skinned potatoes, unpeeled, coarsely chopped

1 large carrot, cut into $1/2$-inch coins

Two $14^1/2$-ounce cans diced tomatoes with garlic, undrained

1 cup uncooked rotini pasta

One 20-ounce package Johnsonville Heat & Serve Italian Sausage, sliced into $1/4$-inch coins

1 zucchini, sliced

$1/2$ cup shredded Parmesan cheese

1. Heat the oil in a stockpot over medium-high heat. Add the onion, and sauté until glossy, 2 to 3 minutes. Add the potatoes and carrot, and sauté for 1 additional minute.

2. Add the tomatoes, 1 cup of water, and the pasta. Cook for 5 minutes. Add the sausage and zucchini. Simmer until the pasta and vegetables are tender and the stew is slightly thickened, about 8 minutes. Place in serving bowls, and top with the cheese.

—— CORN BREAD AND *Smoked Sausage* BAKED STEW ——

With chunks of real Wisconsin Cheddar cheese, our Beddar with Cheddar Smoked Sausage is a perennial favorite. Here we're balancing the robustness of the sausage with the delicate sweetness of corn bread. This dish is even better reheated, if it lasts that long. SERVES 6

Two 10^1/2-ounce cans chicken broth

1 cup sliced fresh mushrooms (6 ounces)

^{1}/2 cup fresh broccoli florets

^{1}/2 cup fresh cauliflower florets

1 cup peeled and coarsely chopped Idaho potatoes

1 large red onion, cut into wedges

4 tablespoons cornstarch

1 cup shredded Cheddar cheese

One 16-ounce package Johnsonville Beddar with Cheddar Smoked Sausage, coin-sliced

One 8^1/2-ounce package corn-muffin mix

1. Preheat the oven to 400°F.

2. Place the broth in a large saucepan and bring to a boil over medium heat. Add the mushrooms, broccoli, cauliflower, potatoes, and onion, and simmer for 10 minutes.

3. In a small bowl, whisk together the cornstarch with 4 tablespoons cold water to create a slurry. Stir the slurry into the broth-vegetable mixture, and cook until thickened, about 2 minutes. Stir in ^{1}/2 cup of the cheese and the sausage. Remove from heat, and allow to cool slightly.

4. Spoon the cooled mixture into a greased 2^1/4-quart casserole dish.

5. In a small bowl, prepare the corn-muffin batter according to the package instructions. Add the remaining cheese.

6. Spoon the batter over the surface of the vegetable-sausage mixture. Bake for 20 to 25 minutes, until the corn bread is golden brown.

Soups and Stews

Pasta and Pizza

CREOLE FETTUCCINE

OLD WORLD LASAGNA

BOWTIE PASTA À LA YOU

PIZZA PASTA

SWEET ITALIAN PASTA TOSS

BEAUTIFUL BAKED ZITI

ONE-PAN ITALIAN

REUBEN PIZZA

OLD-FASHIONED PIZZA

PARTY-SIZE CALZONES

SAUSAGE STROMBOLI

Nineteen-fifties beauty queens parade down Sheboygan's main street.

CREOLE *Fettuccine*

Spicy tomato sauce and winding ribbons of fettuccine are simply the backdrop for this dish's real star: the distinctively flavored Hot Italian Links. You may also use Johnsonville Italian Ground Sausage for this recipe. SERVES 6

One 19.76-ounce package Johnsonville Hot Italian Links, casings removed, or Italian Ground Sausage
Two 14^1/$_2$-ounce cans diced tomatoes, undrained
^{1}/$_3$ cup tomato paste
1 green bell pepper, julienned
Hot pepper sauce
One 9-ounce package refrigerated fresh fettuccine
^{1}/$_3$ cup shredded Parmesan cheese

1. In a large skillet, cook and crumble the sausage over medium heat until browned, 8 to 10 minutes. Drain.

2. In a large saucepan, combine the sausage, tomatoes, tomato paste, bell pepper, and sauce to taste. Bring to a boil over high heat. Reduce heat to medium, and simmer for 5 to 7 minutes.

3. Meanwhile, prepare the fettuccine according to the package instructions. Drain.

4. Pour the sauce over the fettuccine, and top with the cheese.

Even animals dressed in finery to attend Brat Days of yesteryear.

Lasagna

This is hands down the best lasagna you'll ever make. With our spicy Hot Italian Links (or use 1 pound Johnsonville Hot Italian Ground Sausage), ground beef, four cheeses, onion, garlic, and marinara, this flavor-packed dish is sure to impress even the most discriminating palate. It's filling enough on its own, and even better with a simple side salad, crusty bread, and a glass of Chianti. Buon appetito! SERVES 6 TO 8

2 tablespoons olive oil

1 large yellow onion, diced

1 tablespoon minced garlic

5 Johnsonville Hot Italian Links, casings removed

1 pound ground beef

One 32-ounce container ricotta cheese

8 ounces feta cheese

4 cups shredded mozzarella cheese

2 cups freshly grated Parmesan cheese

2 large eggs, lightly beaten

1 teaspoon dried oregano

$1/2$ teaspoon dried thyme

1 teaspoon freshly ground black pepper

10 ounces fresh spinach, chopped

One 7-ounce jar roasted red peppers, chopped

2 tablespoons dried basil

1 pound no-boil or cooked lasagna noodles

Two 26-ounce jars pasta sauce

1. Heat the oil in a large sauté pan over medium heat. Add the onion and garlic, and sauté until glossy but not browned, 1 to 2 minutes. Remove from the pan and set aside, reserving the pan, and allow to cool.

2. In the same pan in which you cooked the onion and garlic, brown the sausage and ground beef. Drain.

3. In a medium bowl, place the ricotta, feta, 3 cups of the mozzarella, 1 cup of the Parmesan, the eggs, oregano, thyme, and pepper. Mix well to combine.

4. In a large bowl, combine the spinach, onions and garlic, roasted peppers, and basil.

5. Preheat the oven to 350°F.

Beauty queens await the crowning of the Brat Days queen.

6. Place four noodles, overlapping the edges, in the bottom of a 9-by-13-inch baking dish. Cover with 1¹/₄ cups of the pasta sauce. Layer 1 cup of the beef-sausage mixture over the sauce. Layer 2 cups of the cheese-egg mixture over the beef-sausage mixture. Layer 1 cup of the spinach mixture over the cheese-egg mixture. Top with noodles. Repeat these steps until all the ingredients are used. Top with the remaining mozzarella and Parmesan cheeses.

7. Bake for 1 hour, or until heated through. Allow to sit 15 minutes before cutting and serving.

Pasta and Pizza

Bowtie Pasta
À LA YOU

"Farfalle," which means "butterflies," is the Italian name for bowtie pasta. Their fun shape and substantial size make them perfect for experimenting with a wide array of toppings and sauces. We've provided some ingredient suggestions here, but we encourage you to try your own additions, such as $1/2$ cup red wine added to the vegetables while sautéing, chopped scallions or roasted bell pepper as garnish, or shredded Asiago cheese as a topping. Make it your own.

SERVES 4 TO 6

5 Johnsonville Mild, Sweet, or Hot Italian Links
One 16-ounce package uncooked farfalle pasta
3 tablespoons olive oil
3 garlic cloves, minced
1 medium yellow onion, cut into small wedges
1 zucchini, sliced $1/4$ inch thick
15 cherry tomatoes, halved
Salt
Freshly ground black pepper

1. Place the links in a very large skillet, and cook according to the package instructions.

2. Meanwhile, prepare the pasta according to the package instructions. Drain.

3. When the links are cooked, remove them from the pan; reserve the drippings and the pan. Slice the links into $1/2$-inch pieces.

4. Add the oil and garlic to the drippings, and sauté over low heat until the garlic releases its flavor but does not begin to brown, about 30 seconds. Add the onion, zucchini, and tomatoes, and sauté until the onion and zucchini are tender-crisp, about 2 minutes. Add the sausage pieces, and cook until they are warmed, about 1 additional minute. Add the pasta, and toss well to combine. Season to taste with salt and pepper. Serve immediately.

The crowning of Miss Bratwurst
Day in Sheboygan, Wisconsin.

PIZZA *Pasta*

All the great taste of pizza—in a pasta. This is a perfect meal for those nights when you're craving a great dish but are too tired to prepare something complicated. You may also use Johnsonville Italian Ground Sausage for this recipe. SERVES 6

One 19.76-ounce package Johnsonville Mild Italian Links, casings removed, or Italian Ground Sausage
8 ounces uncooked rotini pasta
One 15-ounce jar pizza sauce
$1/2$ cup shredded Parmesan cheese
$1/3$ cup chopped green bell pepper
$1/4$ cup sliced black olives
$1^1/2$ cups shredded mozzarella cheese

1. Preheat the oven to 400°F.

2. In a large skillet, cook and crumble the sausage over medium heat until browned, 8 to 10 minutes. Drain.

3. Prepare the pasta according to the package instructions. Drain.

4. In a large bowl, combine the sausage, pasta, sauce, and Parmesan cheese. Place in a greased 12-by-8-inch baking dish. Top with the pepper and olives. Sprinkle with the mozzarella cheese, and bake for 20 to 25 minutes, until heated through.

— SWEET *Italian* PASTA TOSS —

Sweet Italian Pasta Toss is a simple, satisfying meal perfect for cooks of all skill levels. It looks great when served family-style in a simple white dish. The sauce also works well on angel hair pasta. SERVES 6

One 19.76-ounce package Johnsonville Mild Italian Links
One 16-ounce package uncooked rigatoni pasta
3 tablespoons olive oil
2 garlic cloves, minced
1 large red bell pepper, coarsely chopped
One 26-ounce jar pasta sauce
2 tablespoons chopped fresh parsley

1. Prepare the links according to the package instructions. Allow to cool slightly, and then coin-slice. Keep warm.

2. Prepare the pasta according to the package instructions. Drain and keep warm.

3. In a very large sauté pan, heat the oil. Add the garlic, and sauté for 30 seconds. Add the pepper, and sauté until crisp-tender, 3 to 4 minutes. Add the sausage and sauce and heat through.

4. Toss the sausage mixture with the pasta. Serve warm, topped with parsley.

BEAUTIFUL
Baked Ziti

The garlicky, meaty aroma of this dish will entice your family long be-fore it is time to eat. Unlike a traditional ziti, Beautiful Baked Ziti is cov-ered with slices of garlic bread and topped with mozzarella, tomato slices, and basil leaves.

Instead of coin-slicing the sausage, you may wish to remove the casings and cook and crumble it. Though the dish will lack the big, juicy slices as presented her, great sau-sage flavor will be distributed throughout the ziti. It's a matter of personal preference, and in either case you can't go wrong.

SERVES 6 TO 8

One 19.76-ounce package
    Johnsonville Mild, Sweet,
    or Hot Italian Links
$2^1/4$ cups uncooked penne or
    rigatoni pasta
One 26-ounce jar pasta
    sauce
1 tablespoon chopped fresh
    basil
1 tablespoon chopped garlic
4 ounces freshly grated
    Parmesan cheese
$1/4$ teaspoon freshly ground
    black pepper
One 10-ounce package
    frozen garlic bread,
    thawed and cut into
    12 slices
3 cups shredded mozzarella
    cheese
12 slices Roma tomatoes
$1/2$ cup olive oil
12 whole fresh basil leaves

1. Prepare the links according to the package in-structions. Coin-slice.

2. Prepare the pasta according to the package instructions. Drain.

3. Preheat the oven to 400°F.

4. In a large bowl, mix together the sausage, pasta, pasta sauce, $3/4$ cup water, chopped basil, garlic, Parmesan cheese, and pepper. Toss gently. Place this mixture in a greased 9-by-13-inch bak-ing dish.

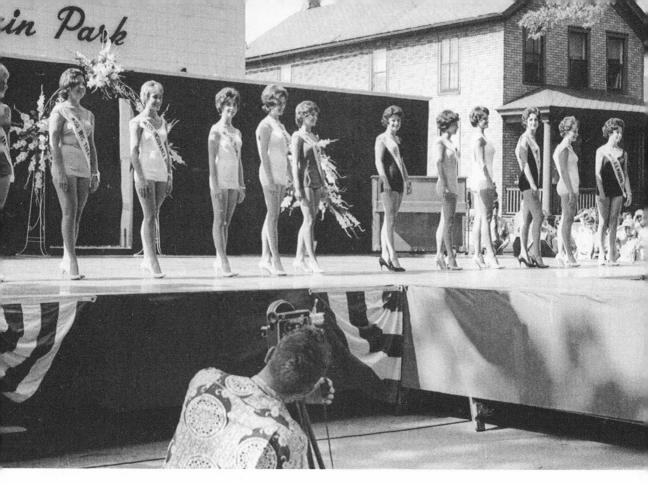

The Brat Days swimsuit competition took place on Sheboygan's main street in the 1950s.

5. Place the slices of garlic bread on top of the sausage mixture, and cover with the mozzarella cheese. Dip the tomato slices in the oil, and place one slice on each piece of bread.

6. Bake for approximately 30 minutes, or until heated through. Tuck an end of a basil leaf under each tomato. Let stand 10 minutes to help the ziti set before slicing and serving.

Pasta and Pizza

One-Pan Italian

We don't know about you, but we're not fans of the fallout from a complicated recipe: towers of dirty dishes covering every bit of counter space that's not littered with empty boxes, jars, and cans. Not only is this recipe delicious, it can be made all in the same pan. If you have any leftovers, it's even better on the second day. SERVES 6

One 19.76-ounce package Johnsonville Mild, Sweet, or Hot Italian Links, casings removed, or Italian Ground Sausage

One 26-ounce jar pasta sauce

8 ounces uncooked spaghetti, broken in half

1. In a large skillet, cook and crumble the sausage over medium heat until browned, 8 to 10 minutes. Drain, reserving the pan and sausage.

2. Bring the sausage up to high heat. Add the sauce, and then fill the jar with water and add that. Bring to a soft boil. Add the pasta, and cook, stirring frequently, until al dente, 7 to 8 minutes.

Reuben Pizza

This unique pizza is based on the classic Reuben sandwich and takes just minutes to prepare. We like it served with suds, and leave the knife and fork in the drawer. MAKES ONE 12-INCH PIZZA

1/4 cup Thousand Island dressing

1/4 cup coarse-ground mustard

One 12-inch prebaked pizza crust

1/4 cup caramelized onions (see page 114)

1/4 cup sauerkraut

1/3 cup coin-sliced Johnsonville Heat & Serve Brats

1/3 cup shredded mozzarella cheese

3/4 cup shredded Swiss cheese

1. Preheat the oven to 350°F.

2. In a small mixing bowl, combine the dressing and mustard. Spread over the crust. Top with the onions, sauerkraut, bratwurst slices, mozzarella cheese, and Swiss cheese.

3. Bake until the cheese is bubbly and golden brown, about 7 minutes.

With a sash and a smile, local women represented the area's sausage companies in the 1957 Bratwurst Day Parade.

JOHNSONVILLE
MEATS
THIELMANN
SAUSAGE CO.
SAUSAGE CO.
ND Sponsored By SAUSAGE MFGS.

OLD-FASHIONED *Pizza*

This recipe includes a crust that must be made a day in advance. Refrigerating it overnight in plastic bags allows the Italian seasoning to infuse the dough with flavor. For a softer crust, substitute flour for cornmeal.

MAKES 2 PIZZAS

CRUST
1 teaspoon Italian seasoning
1 pound frozen white bread
   dough, thawed
2 teaspoons olive oil

PIZZA
2 cups cornmeal
One 28-ounce can whole
   tomatoes, drained and
   sliced in half
3 cups shredded mozzarella
   cheese
1/4 cup sliced black olives
1 cup sliced fresh mushrooms
   (6 ounces)
One 19.76-ounce package
   Johnsonville Hot Italian
   Links, casings removed, or
   Italian Ground Sausage
2 teaspoons Italian seasoning
2 garlic cloves, minced

1. To make the crust: Sprinkle the seasoning over the dough. On a clean surface, knead the dough four or five turns to distribute the seasoning evenly. Cut the dough in half and shape into two balls.

2. Brush the dough balls with the oil. Place them in individual resealable plastic bags, and refrigerate overnight.

3. Remove the dough balls from the refrigerator, and place each, smooth side up, in a large mixing bowl. Cover with plastic wrap, and allow to rise at room temperature until roughly double in size. Remove the wrap, and place your fist in the center of each dough to punch it down. Fold each dough back onto itself four or five times.

4. To make the pizzas: Preheat the oven to 450°F.

5. Sprinkle a clean surface with cornmeal. Roll the doughs out so that each is the size of your pizza stone or pan. Place the doughs on pizza stones or pans, and cover with the tomatoes, sliced side down. Top with

Sonya Thomas, winner of the 2005 Brat Days Brat Eating Contest.

the cheese, olives, and mushrooms. Crumble the uncooked sausage over the cheese and vegetables. Sprinkle with the Italian seasoning and garlic.

6. Bake for 30 minutes, or until the crust is golden brown and the cheese is bubbly.

Pasta and Pizza

— PARTY-SIZE *Calzones* —

Calzones are stuffed pizzas that resemble turnovers and are usually made in individual servings. Perfect for parties, they also make a wonderful after-school snack. SERVES 8

One 19.76-ounce package
  Johnsonville Hot Italian
  Links
1 cup shredded mozzarella
  cheese
1 cup ricotta cheese
1^1/$_2$ teaspoons dried parsley
1 large egg
^{1}/$_2$ garlic clove, minced
^{1}/$_8$ teaspoon onion powder
^{1}/$_8$ teaspoon salt
^{1}/$_8$ teaspoon freshly ground
  black pepper
1 pound frozen white-bread
  dough, thawed
One 15-ounce jar pizza sauce

1. Preheat the oven to 350°F.

2. Place the sausage in a baking dish, and bake for 35 to 40 minutes. Cut into ^{1}/$_4$-inch coins.

3. In a bowl, combine the mozzarella cheese, ricotta cheese, parsley, egg, garlic, onion powder, salt, and pepper.

4. Divide the dough in half. On a lightly floured surface, roll each half into a 12-inch circle.

5. Cover one-half of each circle with the sauce, being careful to leave the edges clean. Cover with the cheese mixture and sausage slices. Fold the clean half of the dough over the covered half to form a half-moon shape. Pinch the edges of the dough to seal the calzones. Transfer to a baking sheet, and bake for 25 to 30 minutes, until lightly golden brown. Cool them slightly before serving.

—— SAUSAGE *Stromboli* ——————————

Philadelphia's version of the calzone, the stromboli is cheese and meat enclosed in pizza or bread dough. We love our Hot Italian Links in our stromboli, but if you can't take the heat, you may want to use our mild or sweet varieties instead. SERVES 6

One 19.76-ounce package Johnsonville Hot Italian Links, casings removed, or Italian Ground Sausage

1 pound frozen white-bread dough, thawed

3 tomatoes, cored and chopped

3 teaspoons olive oil

1 teaspoon Italian seasoning

2 garlic cloves, minced

1$\frac{1}{2}$ cups shredded mozzarella cheese

$\frac{1}{4}$ cup shredded Parmesan cheese

1. Preheat the oven to 400°F.

2. In a large skillet, cook and crumble the sausage over medium heat until browned, 8 to 10 minutes. Drain.

3. On a lightly floured surface, roll the bread dough into a 12-by-16-inch rectangle. Place on a greased baking sheet.

4. In a medium bowl, combine the sausage, tomatoes, 1 teaspoon of the oil, $\frac{1}{2}$ teaspoon of the Italian seasoning, and the garlic. Spread this mixture over the dough rectangle to within 1 inch from the edge; top with the mozzarella cheese. Starting at the long edge, carefully roll the dough jellyroll-style. Tuck the ends under, and make certain that the seam side is down. With a sharp knife, cut four 2-inch-long diagonal slits on the top of the stromboli to vent.

5. In a small bowl, combine the remaining oil with the remaining Italian seasoning. Brush the dough with this mixture. Sprinkle with the Parmesan cheese. Bake for 15 to 20 minutes, or until golden brown. Allow to cool slightly before slicing.

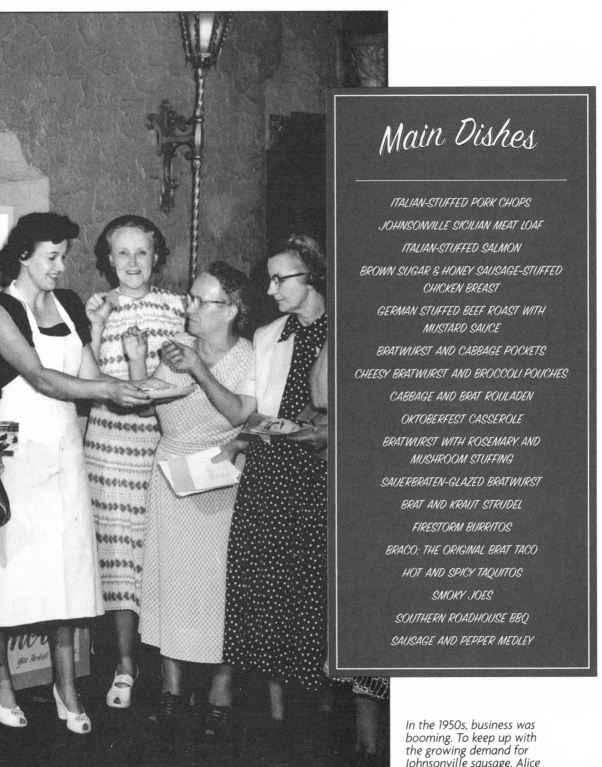

Main Dishes

ITALIAN-STUFFED PORK CHOPS

JOHNSONVILLE SICILIAN MEAT LOAF

ITALIAN-STUFFED SALMON

BROWN SUGAR & HONEY SAUSAGE-STUFFED
CHICKEN BREAST

GERMAN STUFFED BEEF ROAST WITH
MUSTARD SAUCE

BRATWURST AND CABBAGE POCKETS

CHEESY BRATWURST AND BROCCOLI POUCHES

CABBAGE AND BRAT ROULADEN

OKTOBERFEST CASSEROLE

BRATWURST WITH ROSEMARY AND
MUSHROOM STUFFING

SAUERBRATEN-GLAZED BRATWURST

BRAT AND KRAUT STRUDEL

FIRESTORM BURRITOS

BRACO: THE ORIGINAL BRAT TACO

HOT AND SPICY TAQUITOS

SMOKY JOES

SOUTHERN ROADHOUSE BBQ

SAUSAGE AND PEPPER MEDLEY

In the 1950s, business was booming. To keep up with the growing demand for Johnsonville sausage, Alice Stayer recruited local women to assist in sales.

ITALIAN-STUFFED
Pork Chops

In this decadent main course, we stuff butterflied pork chops with Johnsonville Italian sausage, and then add a light and crisp crust of bread crumbs that bakes golden brown and keeps all the flavorful succulence inside. It's an impressive presentation that is surprisingly simple to make.

Based on personal preference, you may use Johnsonville Mild, Sweet, or Hot Italian Links for this recipe. SERVES 4

One 19.76-ounce package
   Johnsonville Italian Links,
   casings removed, or Italian
   Ground Sausage
1/2 cup shredded Romano
   cheese
Four 1-inch-thick pork chops,
   butterflied
1 cup all-purpose flour
1 large egg
1 cup milk
1 1/2 cups Italian bread
   crumbs
Nonstick pan spray
2 tablespoons lemon juice

1. Preheat the oven to 375°F.

2. Place the sausage in a large bowl. Add the cheese. Mix well to combine.

3. Stuff each pork chop with the sausage-cheese mixture, folding the pork chops over to create a sandwich.

4. Place the flour in a shallow dish. Place the egg and milk in a second shallow dish, and whisk to combine. Place the bread crumbs in a third shallow dish. Dredge the pork chops in the flour. Dip the pork chops in the milk-egg mixture and completely coat. Dredge the coated pork chops in the bread crumbs.

5. Coat a baking sheet with the nonstick spray. Place the pork chops on the sheet, and bake for 45 minutes. Turn and bake for 15 additional minutes, or until the chops have an internal temperature of 180°F. Drizzle the chops with lemon juice.

Sicilian Meat Loaf

Remember your mother's meat loaf? Dry, bland hamburger disguised with ketchup? This ain't it. By adding Johnsonville Hot Italian Links to hamburger, you'll get a more flavorful, full-bodied dish that your own kids will remember fondly.

Depending on how you like it, you may use Johnsonville Mild, Sweet, or Hot Italian Links for this recipe. It is excellent served with a side of warm marinara sauce. If you're lucky enough to have some left over, it makes a great cold sandwich. SERVES 6 TO 8

4 Johnsonville Italian Links, casings removed, or one 16-ounce package Johnsonville Italian Ground Sausage

1 pound lean ground beef

$3/4$ cup bread crumbs

$3/4$ cup milk

1 large egg

$1/2$ cup minced celery

$1/2$ cup minced yellow onion

4 garlic cloves, crushed

2 teaspoons Worcestershire sauce

$1/2$ teaspoon dried basil

1 teaspoon dried oregano

$1/2$ teaspoon salt

$1/2$ teaspoon freshly ground black pepper

6 ounces ham slices

4 ounces mozzarella cheese, shredded

4 ounces provolone cheese, shredded

1. Preheat the oven to 350°F.

2. In a large bowl, combine the sausage and beef.

3. In a small bowl, combine the bread crumbs, milk, and egg. Allow to sit until all the liquid is absorbed, about 5 minutes. Add this mixture to the sausage-beef mixture. Add the celery, onion, garlic, Worcestershire sauce, basil, oregano, salt, and pepper, and mix well to combine.

4. Press the mixture into a baking dish. Top with the ham slices. Sprinkle with the cheeses, and bake for 1 hour, or until cooked through. Allow to stand for 15 minutes prior to serving.

Main Dishes

—— ITALIAN-STUFFED *Salmon* ——

Based on personal preference, you may use Johnsonville Mild, Sweet, or Hot Italian Links for this recipe. Italian-Stuffed Salmon is excellent served with fettuccine and a simple mixed-greens salad. SERVES 8

1 tablespoon chopped fresh basil

4 tablespoons olive oil

3 garlic cloves, minced

Two 1-pound salmon fillets

One 19.76-ounce package Johnsonville Italian Links, casings removed, or Italian Ground Sausage

1/4 cup black olive paste

4 ounces white or yellow sharp Cheddar, shredded

6 ounces red bell pepper, roasted (see page 46) and diced

Salt

Freshly ground black pepper

4 sheets frozen puff pastry, thawed

Egg wash (1 large egg whisked with 1/2 cup cool water)

1. Place the basil, oil, and garlic in a small mixing bowl. Whisk well to combine.

2. Place the salmon fillets in the marinade, and allow to marinate in the refrigerator for at least 1 hour.

3. Preheat the oven to 400°F. Remove the fillets from the marinade, and pat dry with paper towels or a clean kitchen cloth.

4. Place the sausage in a large bowl. Add the olive paste, cheese, bell peppers, salt, and pepper. Blend well.

5. Place one fillet on a sheet of puff pastry. Top with half of the meat mixture. Brush the edges of the puff pastry with the egg wash. Place a second sheet of puff pastry over the salmon, lining up its edges with that of the bottom sheet. Using a fork, gently crimp the edges together. Repeat with the second fillet.

6. Place on an ungreased baking sheet, and bake for 40 to 50 minutes, until fully cooked and golden brown. Let stand 20 minutes before slicing on an angle and serving.

BROWN SUGAR & HONEY
Sausage-Stuffed
CHICKEN BREAST

This is an elegant, sweet-and-savory main course appropriate for a lavish dinner party or an enjoyable night in. Chicken breasts are stuffed with our famous Brown Sugar & Honey Links, and then covered with a honey-cinnamon glaze and baked until crunchy on the outside and moist and tender on the inside. It is sure to become one of your most popular recipes. SERVES 4

Four 5-ounce boneless,
   skinless chicken breasts,
   butterflied
Salt
Freshly ground black pepper
12 Johnsonville Brown Sugar
   & Honey Links
$1/2$ cup honey
1 teaspoon cinnamon
2 cups coarse bread crumbs

1. Preheat the oven to 400°F.

2. Season the inside of the chicken breasts with salt and pepper. Remove the casings from three of the links. Place this sausage meat on one-half of the inside of one butterflied breast. Fold the clean side of the breast over the covered side to create a sandwich shape. Repeat with the remaining sausages and breasts.

3. In a small bowl, combine the honey and cinnamon. Spoon this mixture over the stuffed breasts.

4. Place the bread crumbs in a shallow dish. Very carefully dredge the stuffed breasts in the crumbs. Place in a baking dish, and bake for 35 minutes, or until the breasts have an internal temperature of 165°F or above.

Locals step up to the condiment counter at the 1958 Brat Days.

German Stuffed Beef Roast
WITH MUSTARD SAUCE

This recipe harks back to Wisconsin's German roots. Beef loin roast is stuffed with our famous Original Bratwurst, and then tied and slow-cooked until tender. Served with a brown mustard sauce, it is an impressive dish for a dinner party.

A helpful tip for shaping the sausage: dip your hands in cold water to keep the meat from sticking to your hands. You will need 3 feet of butcher's string for trussing the roast. Jellyroll-cut beef roast tip may be used in place of the loin roast. SERVES 8 TO 10

3 pounds boneless beef loin roast, jellyroll-cut

2 tablespoons Tabasco Garlic Pepper Sauce

2 tablespoons crushed garlic

2 carrots, cut into thin strips

2 celery ribs, cut into thin strips

1 apple, unpeeled, cored and shredded

5 Johnsonville Original Bratwurst Links, casings removed

$1/2$ cup coarse-ground mustard

Three $10^1/2$-ounce cans beef broth

1. Preheat the oven to 350°F.

2. Rub the top, bottom, and sides of the roast with the Garlic Pepper Sauce. Rub the top of the roast with the crushed garlic; cover with the carrots, celery, and apple.

3. Shape the bratwurst meat into an oblong shape the same length as the roast. Place on top of the carrots, celery, and apple. Roll the roast jellyroll-style, and tie it together so that it maintains its shape during the cooking process. Brush with 4 tablespoons of the mustard.

4. Place the roast in a baking dish and bake for 2 hours, or until the internal temperature reaches 180°F.

Sheboygan-area men enjoy Johnsonville brats and beer at a 1960s Brat Days.

5. To make the mustard sauce: Meanwhile, place the broth in a large pot and bring to a boil over high heat. Add the remaining 4 tablespoons of the mustard and reduce by one-third.

6. Remove the roast from the oven. Let stand 10 minutes. Remove the string, and then slice into $^{1}/_{2}$-inch slices. Serve with the mustard sauce.

Anything but Common Condiments: Flavored Mustards

Anyone who's eaten perfectly seasoned Johnsonville brats knows that they're great on their own. But if you'd like to mix things up a bit, Johnsonville Executive Chef Mike Zeller is a fan of flavored mustards and shares his five favorites here:

AMBER GARLIC MUSTARD WITH DILL

1 tablespoon unsalted butter
2 garlic cloves, crushed
1 tablespoon mustard seed
$^1/_2$ cup dark beer
1 teaspoon mustard powder
$1^1/_2$ teaspoons dried dillweed
$^1/_2$ cup horseradish mustard

Melt the butter in a saucepan. Add the garlic and mustard seed, and cook over low heat for 3 minutes. Add the beer, mustard powder, and dillweed, and reduce by half. Blend this mixture with the mustard, and refrigerate overnight in an airtight container.

DRUNKEN RED PEPPER MUSTARD WITH JALAPEÑO

1 tablespoon mustard seed
2 teaspoons mustard powder
$1/2$ teaspoon red pepper flakes
1 teaspoon apple cider vinegar
$1/2$ cup dark beer
1 tablespoon chopped fresh chives
2 roasted jalapeños in liquid, drained
One 8-ounce jar coarse-ground mustard

In a small mixing bowl, combine the mustard seed, mustard powder, pepper flakes, vinegar, and beer. Refrigerate overnight in an airtight container. Heat the liquid in a medium saucepan over high heat until it is reduced by one-half. Add the chives, jalapeños, and mustard. Store refrigerated in an airtight container.

CHUNKY CRANBERRY MUSTARD

The procedure for roasting bell peppers is the same as that for banana peppers. See page 46 for instructions, or use roasted bell peppers in a jar, draining them before use.

$^1/_2$ cup whiskey
$1^1/_2$ cups cranberries
1 medium yellow onion, diced
1 red bell pepper, roasted and diced
1 yellow bell pepper, roasted and diced
1 green bell pepper, roasted and diced
2 tablespoons balsamic vinegar
$^1/_2$ cup frozen orange-juice concentrate
$^1/_2$ cup coarse-ground mustard

1. Simmer the whiskey, cranberries, and onion in a medium saucepan over medium-low heat until the liquid is reduced by one-half.

2. Allow to cool slightly, and then pulse in the blender for 3 to 5 seconds, until the berries are sliced but still chunky. Place in a medium mixing bowl. Add the red bell pepper, yellow bell pepper, green bell pepper, vinegar, juice concentrate, and mustard, and blend well. Store refrigerated in an airtight container.

SUN-DRIED TOMATO AND BASIL MUSTARD WITH FETA

1 tablespoon unsalted butter
2 teaspoons chopped fresh basil
1 garlic clove, crushed
$^1/_2$ cup diced Roma tomatoes
1 cup sun-dried tomatoes, diced
$^1/_2$ cup dark beer
One 8-ounce jar coarse-ground mustard
$^1/_4$ cup crumbled feta cheese

1. Melt the butter in a small saucepan over low heat. Add the basil, garlic, Roma tomatoes, and sun-dried tomatoes, and cook for 2 minutes.

2. Add the beer, and reduce by one-half. Remove from heat, and allow to cool slightly.

3. Add the mustard and cheese, and blend well to combine. Store refrigerated in an airtight container.

WHISKEY AND BLACK PEPPERCORN MUSTARD

The procedure for roasting bell peppers is the same as that for banana peppers. See page 46 for instructions, or use roasted bell peppers in a jar, draining them before use.

1 tablespoon black peppercorns
$^1/_2$ cup whiskey
1 red bell pepper, roasted
1 yellow bell pepper, roasted
1 green bell pepper, roasted
1 medium yellow onion
$^1/_2$ cup coarse-ground mustard

1. Place the peppercorns and whiskey in a medium saucepan. Simmer on low until reduced by one-half.

2. Cut each bell pepper and the onion in half. Place one-half of each in a blender with one-half of the peppercorns and whiskey and the mustard, and blend until smooth. Pour the mixture into a bowl.

3. Dice the remaining bell peppers and onion. Add to the bowl, and mix well to combine. Store refrigerated in an airtight container.

Bratwurst and Cabbage
POCKETS

A recipe inspired by Johnsonville Executive Chef Michael Zeller's child-hood, Bratwurst and Cabbage Pockets is a fun twist on the traditional Germanic flavors of sausage, cabbage, and onions. SERVES 4 TO 6

12 Johnsonville Original Bratwurst Links, casings removed

3 pounds green cabbage, shredded and blanched

3 large yellow onions, sliced and sautéed

2 tablespoons salt

3 tablespoons freshly ground black pepper

Two 1-pound loaves frozen white-bread dough, thawed

1. Brown the bratwurst meat according to the package instructions, and drain.

2. Preheat the oven to 350°F.

3. In a large bowl, combine the sausage, cabbage, onions, salt, and pepper to make the filling.

4. Cut each dough loaf in half. Roll out each piece so that it is approximately 18 by 4 inches.

5. Place $1/2$-cup mounds of the sausage mixture onto one sheet of dough, leaving 6 inches between the mounds. Brush water on the exposed dough. Line up one end of a second sheet of dough and carefully drape it over the filling, pressing down between the mounds to seal and remove air pockets. Repeat with the remaining sheets. Cut the dough between the mounds, and crimp the edges of each with a fork.

6. Place on a baking sheet, and bake for 12 to 15 minutes, until golden brown.

CHEESY
Bratwurst and Broccoli
POUCHES

If you've never tried the combination of bratwurst and broccoli, you're in for a treat. Here plump and juicy sausage, sautéed onion, tender-crisp broccoli florets, and melted American cheese are enveloped in a delicate puff-pastry pouch. To mix up the flavor of these tasty packages, experiment with the cheese of your choice. We love Swiss, Asiago, or smoked provolone. SERVES 6 TO 8

One 19.76-ounce package Johnsonville Original Bratwurst Links
1 tablespoon unsalted butter
1 large yellow onion, sliced
1^1/$_2$ cups fresh broccoli florets
1^1/$_2$ cups shredded American cheese
One 17.25-ounce package frozen puff pastry, thawed and cut into 4-by-4-inch squares

1. Preheat the oven to 350°F.

2. Cook the links according to the package instructions. Slice into ^{1}/4-inch coins.

3. Melt the butter in a large skillet over medium heat. Add the onion, and sauté until lightly golden.

4. Bring a medium saucepan of water to a boil. Blanch the broccoli until tender-crisp, about 5 minutes. Drain well.

5. Divide the sausage coins, broccoli, onion, and cheese evenly among the pastry squares. Wet the edges of each square with water. Bring the corners of the pastry together, creating a pouch. Pinch the top to seal.

6. Place the pouches on an ungreased baking sheet, and bake for 12 minutes, or until golden brown.

Johnsonville Chunky Brat Chili, page 68

Old World Lasagna, page 80

Beautiful Baked Ziti, page 86

Southern Roadhouse BBQ, page 128

Sausage and Pepper Medley, page 129

Italian Chicken and Sausage Salad, page 132

*Chipotle Shrimp, New Orleans–Style Sausage,
and Pineapple Skewers, page 170*

Summer Sausage S'Mores, page 176

Brat Days 101

By now you've figured out that Sheboygan County, Wisconsin, is bonkers for bratwursts. Just how bonkers? Enough to hold a three-day event in their honor.

Since 1953, Brat Days have celebrated the splendor of sausage with the crowning of the Brat Days queen and fun for all ages. Below, a brief Brat Days tutorial:

- More than 2.5 million people have attended Brat Days.

- In an average year, seventy thousand brats are consumed in less than thirty-six hours.

- Today, exotic menu items such as brat egg rolls and brat tacos are featured alongside the Traditional Sheboygan Double Brat.

- The event has raised more than $150,000 for charity over the past decade.

- Sonya Thomas set the brat-eating world record in 2005, devouring thirty-five brats in just ten minutes. She smashed the previous record of nineteen and a half brats, which was set in 2004.

- The Johnsonville Brat Days Brat Eating Contest features "naked" brats—no bun, no condiments—just the incomparable flavor of Johnsonville.

CABBAGE AND BRAT *Rouladen*

This German-inspired dish is best cooked on the grill, using aluminum-foil baking pans, but you may also prepare it in a 350°F oven, using conventional baking dishes.

The secret to this recipe's sweetness is caramelized onions. Think you don't know how to caramelize onions? Think again. If you've ever been distracted by the telephone or your children while sautéing onions and returned to the stovetop to find them browned, that's caramelizing. When cooked long enough, onions release their natural sugars, and the result is an unexpected addition to savory dishes such as this. It takes a bit of time, but trust us, it's well worth the effort. SERVES 10

Two 19.76-ounce packages Johnsonville Original Bratwurst Links

3 tablespoons olive oil

2 large yellow onions, thinly sliced

4 ounces coarse-ground mustard

10 leaves green cabbage, blanched

One 32-ounce bottle spicy Bloody Mary mix

1. Prepare the links according to the package instructions. Set aside.

2. Heat the oil in a large sauté pan over high heat. Add the onions, and sauté until they begin to caramelize, 8 to 10 minutes.

3. Heat the grill. Brush mustard on one side of each cabbage leaf. Place about $1/4$ cup caramelized onion inside each leaf, and top with a link. Fold the leaves around the links, rolling tightly and tucking in the ends.

4. Place the cabbage rolls, seam side down, in a 9-by-13-inch aluminum-foil baking pan. Pour the Bloody Mary mix over the rolls. Heat on a grill for 30 minutes, or until cooked through.

OKTOBERFEST *Casserole*

This comforting casserole celebrates the flavors of Germany during Oktoberfest. Though the beer flavor is just a whisper in this dish, using berry-, honey-, or wheat-flavored beer does affect its flavor. Try some different flavors and find your favorite.

We like leaving the links whole for a more rustic presentation, but you could slice them into 1-inch pieces after they're browned. SERVES 4

One 19.76-ounce package Johnsonville Original Bratwurst Links
2 tablespoons unsalted butter
1 medium yellow onion, sliced
1 Granny Smith apple, unpeeled, cored and wedged
1 pound red-skinned potatoes, unpeeled, cubed
One 27-ounce jar sauerkraut
One 14$^1/_2$-ounce can chicken broth
1 teaspoon caraway seed
$^3/_4$ cup beer
Salt
Freshly ground black pepper
$^1/_4$ cup sliced scallions, white and green parts

1. Preheat the oven to 350°F.

2. Place the links in a flameproof casserole dish, and brown them on the stovetop over high heat. Remove the links, reserving the casserole and the links.

3. To the same casserole in which you browned the links, add the butter, onion, and apple, and cook over medium-high heat until the onion is transparent, about 5 minutes.

4. Add the potatoes, sauerkraut, broth, caraway seed, and beer. Stir to combine. Add the links. Season to taste with salt and pepper.

5. Cover the casserole, and bake for 45 minutes to 1 hour, until the casserole is warmed through and the liquid is reduced. Top with the sliced scallions and serve.

Bratwurst
WITH ROSEMARY AND MUSHROOM STUFFING

Our sausage is so perfectly seasoned that, as Ralph C. Stayer, Johnsonville's CEO, is fond of saying, "The best thing to put on a Johnsonville bratwurst is your teeth." But sometimes even a bratwurst likes to get dressed up. In this unique recipe, we hinge-slice brats and top them with a moist herb-and-bacon stuffing that gets baked golden brown.

To make fine cracker crumbs easily, place the saltines in a resealable plastic bag and cover with a kitchen towel. Gently roll over the bag with a rolling pin until the crackers are finely ground. SERVES 4 TO 8

8 Johnsonville Original Bratwurst Links
1 tablespoon olive oil
1 small yellow onion, diced
$1/2$ cup diced green bell pepper
3 tablespoons chopped fresh parsley
$1/2$ teaspoon chopped fresh rosemary
One $10^3/4$-ounce can condensed cream-of-mushroom soup
$1^1/4$ cups finely ground saltine crackers (about 45 crackers)
$1/4$ pound bacon slices, fried crisp, drained, and chopped

1. Preheat the oven to 425°F.

2. Prepare the links according to the package instructions. Allow to cool.

3. Heat the oil in a large sauté pan over medium heat. Add the onion, pepper, parsley, and rosemary, and sauté until the onion and pepper are crisp-tender, about 2 minutes. Add the soup and $3/4$ cup of the ground crackers and blend well.

4. Being careful not to slice all the way through, hinge-cut the bratwursts lengthwise so that they open flat. Place them in a baking dish. Cover with the vegetable-soup mixture. Sprinkle with the remaining crackers and the bacon. Bake uncovered for 25 minutes, or until the stuffing is golden brown.

— SAUERBRATEN-GLAZED *Bratwurst* —

German for "sour roast," sauerbraten is a traditional German dish made by marinating beef in a sweet-and-sour sauce for at least 48 hours, and then slow-cooking it until fork-tender. You may wish to serve this dish with traditional sauerbraten accompaniments: potato dumplings, boiled new potatoes, or spätzle. SERVES 6

12 Johnsonville Original
   Bratwurst Links
1 cup sugar
2 cups vinegar
3 stalks celery, diced
$1/4$ cup diced green bell
   pepper
1 small carrot, diced
1 small yellow onion, diced
1 tablespoon pickling spice
15 gingersnaps, crushed

1. Grill the links according to the package instructions. Keep warm.

2. Place the sugar, vinegar, 2 cups water, celery, pepper, carrot, onion, and spice in a large saucepan. Bring to a boil over medium heat. Allow to simmer for 15 minutes.

3. Strain the liquid with a fine-mesh sieve, discarding the solids. Return the liquid to the pan, and bring to a boil over medium heat. Add one-half of the gingersnaps, whisking thoroughly. Add the remaining gingersnaps, and whisk until the liquid is thickened and the consistency is smooth, about 1 minute.

4. Place 2 bratwursts on each serving plate, and top with the sauce.

A large crowd gathers for a 1950s Brat Days celebration.

Qmach's

unn-Bush
SHOES

JAYCEE BRATW

SATURDAY AUGUST 7th — CONTINUOUS

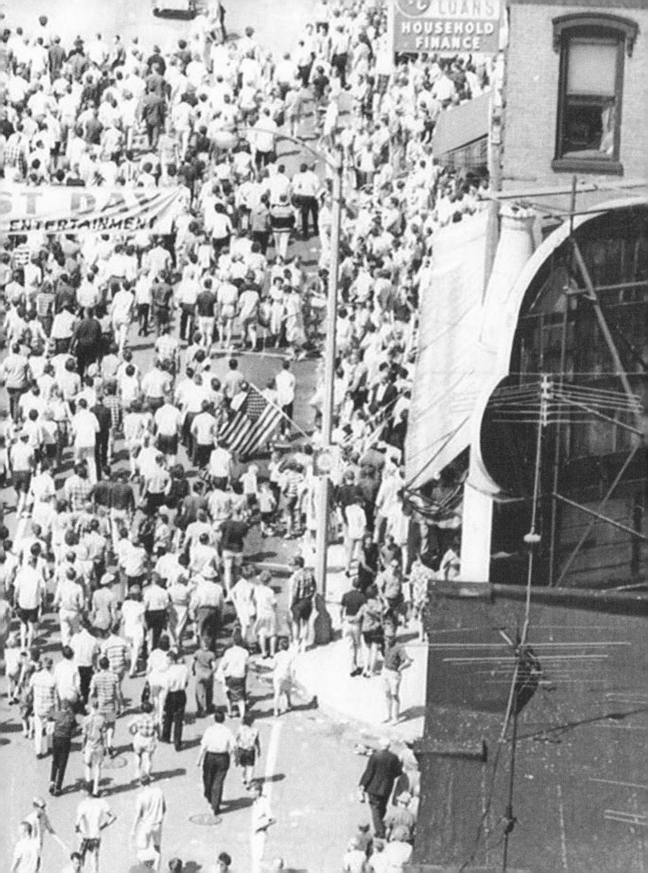

BRAT AND KRAUT
Strudel

Another of our favorite savory strudels, this one is decidedly German.

MAKES TWO 12-BY-2^1/$_2$-INCH STRUDELS

One 19.76-ounce package
 Johnsonville Original
 Bratwurst Links
2 tablespoons unsalted
 butter
1 medium yellow onion,
 sliced
One 14-ounce can
 sauerkraut, drained
^{1}/$_2$ cup sour cream
^{1}/$_2$ teaspoon minced garlic
^{1}/$_2$ teaspoon dillweed
^{1}/$_2$ teaspoon caraway seed
Salt
Freshly ground black pepper
2 sheets frozen puff pastry,
 thawed
2 cups shredded Muenster
 cheese
2 tablespoons poppy seeds
2 tablespoons sesame seeds

1. Preheat the oven to 450°F.

2. Prepare the links according to the package in-structions. Cool slightly, and then cut into half-moon slices.

3. In a large sauté pan, melt the butter over medium heat. Add the onion, and sauté until caramelized, 8 to 10 minutes. Add the sausage and sauerkraut; heat through.

4. In a small bowl, combine the sour cream, gar-lic, dill, and caraway. Season to taste with salt and pepper.

5. Line two baking sheets with parchment paper or silicone nonstick baking pads. Unfold one sheet of puff pastry on each baking sheet. Spread the sour-cream mixture over each pastry sheet to within ^{1}/$_2$ inch of the edge. Spoon the sausage mixture down the center of each pastry sheet. Top with the cheese. Lightly brush the edges with water. Fold the long pastry side of each sheet over the filling and pinch the ends to-gether to seal.

6. With a sharp knife, pierce the strudels to create steam vents. Brush the tops of the strudels with water. Sprinkle with the poppy and sesame seeds.

7. Bake for 30 to 35 minutes, until golden brown. Let stand 10 minutes before slicing.

What the Heck's a Fry-Out?

The aroma of grilling bratwursts permeates the crisp air on autumn weekends in Sheboygan County, as organizations take to quaint timber stands called "brat hauses" and "fry out" to raise money for charitable causes.

What the heck's frying out? you may ask. While the rest of the country grills or has a backyard barbecue, we fry out.

— FIRESTORM *Burritos* ——————

Spicy sausage, cool sour-cream sauce, fresh veggies, and tender tortillas make this tasty dish a hit. Add some nachos on the side and you've got a fiesta!

If you can't locate lime-and-garlic salsa in your area, substitute the salsa of your choice. SERVES 8

1 cup sour cream
2¹/₂ teaspoons Tabasco
    Chipotle Pepper Sauce
1 heaping tablespoon
    chopped fresh cilantro
8 links Johnsonville Hot 'n
    Spicy Bratwurst
Eight 10- or 12-inch tortillas
1 jar lime-and-garlic salsa
1 green bell pepper, finely
    diced
1 red bell pepper, finely
    diced
1 tomato, diced
1 bunch scallions, white and
    light green parts only,
    sliced
1 red onion, diced
1¹/₂ cups shredded Monterey
    Jack cheese

1. Heat the grill.

2. To make the sauce: Blend the sour cream, pepper sauce, and cilantro. Chill.

3. Grill the links according to the package instructions, and keep warm.

4. Heat the tortillas according to the package instructions. Spread about 2 tablespoons of the sour-cream sauce on each tortilla, and top with 2 tablespoons of the salsa. Place a link on each tortilla. Cover with 1 tablespoon each of the green bell pepper, red bell pepper, tomato, scallions, and red onion. Sprinkle with the cheese. Roll and serve.

Johnsonville
BIG TASTE OF SAUSAGE COOKBOOK
122

— BRACO: THE *Original* BRAT TACO —

With mouth-watering Johnsonville Original Bratwurst playing the role of ground beef, and satisfying pita pockets serving as taco shells, this fun presentation puts a new spin on traditional tacos. Strips of tender and juicy grilled bratwurst are also a wonderful twist for fajitas.

SERVES 4 TO 6

One 19.76-ounce package Johnsonville Original Bratwurst Links
One 16-ounce container sour cream
2 dashes hot sauce
2 garlic cloves, crushed
2 tablespoons diced red bell pepper
2 tablespoons diced yellow bell pepper
2 tablespoons diced green bell pepper
Juice and pulp of 1 lime
$1/2$ teaspoon minced fresh cilantro
3 tablespoons olive oil
One 12-ounce package 12-inch pita breads
1 large tomato, thinly sliced
1 medium yellow onion, thinly sliced
1 avocado, thinly sliced

1. Grill the links according to the package instructions. Slice each lengthwise into four strips. Keep warm.

2. In a medium bowl, combine the sour cream, hot sauce, garlic, red bell pepper, yellow bell pepper, green bell pepper, lime juice and pulp, and cilantro.

3. Brush the pitas with the oil. Grill until crisp around the edges.

4. Spread about 2 tablespoons of the sour-cream mixture inside each pita. Add two or three slices of the tomato, onion, and avocado. Top with three or four brat strips each and serve immediately.

Main Dishes

Big taste from a small town in a big city: Ralph C. Stayer serves a brat from a Johnsonville sausage stand in Tokyo, Japan.

Hot and Spicy TAQUITOS

This simple and flavorful Mexican-inspired dish is wonderful served with guacamole, sliced black olives, salsa, and a side of sour cream flavored with cumin or chipotle seasoning.

Zest is the thin, colored outer layer of citrus peel. It can be removed with a citrus zester or fine cheese-grater. SERVES 10

One 19.76-ounce package Johnsonville Hot 'n Spicy Bratwurst, casings removed

1/4 cup diced red bell pepper

1/4 cup diced yellow bell pepper

1/4 cup diced green bell pepper

1/4 cup diced red onion

One 10-ounce can diced tomatoes with green chiles, drained

1 tablespoon coarsely chopped fresh cilantro

Zest and juice of 1/2 lime

1 1/4 cups shredded Monterey Jack cheese

Twenty 6-inch flour tortillas

Oil for deep-frying

1. In a large skillet, cook and crumble the sausage over medium heat until browned. Drain. Place the sausage in a large bowl. Add the peppers, onion, tomatoes, cilantro, lime zest and juice, and cheese. Mix well to combine.

2. Place 2 heaping teaspoons of the mixture on one edge of a flour tortilla. Roll jellyroll-style. Place the stuffed taquito, seam side down, in a small baking dish to keep it from unrolling. Repeat with the remaining tortillas, placing the taquitos in the same dish.

3. Heat the oil in a deep-fryer or heavy, deep skillet. When the oil reaches 375°F, plunge the taquitos in batches into the oil until golden brown, about 30 seconds. Drain on paper toweling. Serve immediately.

Smoky JOES

Once you've had Smoky Joes made with Johnsonville Original Bratwurst, you'll never go back to ground beef. For more kick, use our Hot 'n Spicy Bratwurst. You can also use Johnsonville Italian Ground Sausage for this recipe. SERVES 6

One 19.76-ounce package
   Johnsonville Original
   Bratwurst Links, casings
   removed
2 teaspoons olive oil
1 small yellow onion, sliced
1 cup sliced fresh mushrooms
   (6 ounces)
$1^1/_4$ cups barbecue sauce
6 kaiser rolls, split
$1^1/_2$ cups shredded sharp
   Cheddar cheese

1. In a large skillet, cook and crumble the sausage over medium heat until browned. Drain.

2. Heat the oil in a medium saucepan. Add the onion, and sauté until glossy, about 2 minutes. Add the mushrooms, and sauté an additional 3 minutes. Add the sausage and the sauce. Simmer until hot, 5 to 8 minutes.

3. Spoon the sausage mixture onto the bottom half of each roll. Top with the cheese and the top half of the roll.

SOUTHERN *Roadhouse* BBQ

Here we slather our award-winning Heat & Serve Brats with tangy barbecue sauce, top them with cool slaw, and serve them on crusty rolls. Great with potato salad and chips, Southern Roadhouse BBQ is perfect for a casual night in or for a picnic. SERVES 6

3 tablespoons olive oil
1 large yellow onion, thinly sliced
3 garlic cloves, thinly sliced
5 links Johnsonville Heat & Serve Brats, bias-sliced
2 cups barbecue sauce
16 ounces shredded cabbage
16 ounces oil-and-vinegar dressing
6 crusty kaiser rolls, split

1. Heat the oil in a large sauté pan over medium heat. Add the onion and garlic, and sauté until golden, about 2 minutes. Add the sliced bratwurst and barbecue sauce, and cook an additional 3 minutes.

2. Place the cabbage in a large bowl and add the dressing. Mix well to combine.

3. Spoon the BBQ mixture onto the bottom half of each roll. Top with the coleslaw and the top half of the roll.

— SAUSAGE AND *Pepper* MEDLEY —

Carb-conscious? If so, this is your dish. If you are not counting carbs, be sure to have some crusty bread handy. You may use Johnsonville Mild, Sweet, or Hot Italian Links in this recipe. SERVES 6

One 19.76-ounce package
   Johnsonville Italian Links
$1/4$ cup olive oil
2 garlic cloves, crushed
1 red bell pepper, julienned
1 yellow bell pepper,
   julienned
1 green bell pepper, julienned
$1/2$ yellow onion, julienned
One 28-ounce can chopped
   Italian tomatoes with
   herbs
Salt
Freshly ground black pepper
$1/2$ cup freshly grated
   Parmesan cheese

1. Prepare the links according to the package instructions, and bias-slice. Set aside.

2. In a large pan, heat the oil over medium heat. Add the garlic, and sauté for about 30 seconds. Add the red bell pepper, yellow bell pepper, green bell pepper, and onion, and sauté until tender-crisp, about 2 minutes. Add the tomatoes and sausage, and cook for 5 additional minutes. Season to taste and serve. Sprinkle with the cheese.

Salads and *Sides*

ITALIAN CHICKEN AND SAUSAGE SALAD

DANIEL BOULUD'S BRATWURST AND
RED ONION SALAD

WARM CAJUN POTATO SALAD

COOL GARLIC SUMMER PASTA SALAD

JOHNSONVILLE NEW ORLEANS-STYLE SAUSAGE
WITH BEANS AND APPLE

SAUSAGE, PECAN, AND CRANBERRY STUFFING

GRANDMA ALICE'S SAUSAGE STUFFING

BEDDAR WITH CHEDDAR VEGETABLE BAKE

ITALIAN AU GRATIN POTATO BAKE

CREOLE SAUSAGE AND RICE

CAJUN STUFFED PEPPERS

HOLYLAND BEANS

Nearly sixty years after Ralph and Alice Stayer founded the Johnsonville Meat Market, they continue to play a role in the Johnsonville Sausage business.

ITALIAN
Chicken and Sausage
SALAD

Even the most ardent carnivore is sure to be converted by this salad: marinated chicken breast, sautéed vegetables, and juicy Johnsonville Italian Links served warm atop succulent romaine lettuce leaves. You may use the Johnsonville Italian Links of choice. SERVES 6

16 ounces boneless, skinless chicken breast, thinly sliced

6 ounces Italian dressing

16 ounces Johnsonville Italian Links

2 tablespoons olive oil

1 teaspoon chopped garlic

2 cups sliced fresh mushrooms (12 ounces)

10 cherry tomatoes, quartered

4 scallions, white and light green parts only

1 pound romaine lettuce leaves, torn into bite-size pieces

1/2 cup freshly grated Parmesan cheese

1. Marinate the chicken in the dressing for a minimum of 2 hours.

2. Prepare the links according to the package instructions, and bias-slice. Set aside.

3. Heat the oil in a large skillet. Sauté the chicken and garlic for 4 minutes. Add the mushrooms, tomatoes, scallions, and sausage; sauté until hot, about 3 additional minutes.

4. Place the mixture over the lettuce, and top with the cheese. Serve warm.

Bratwurst and Red Onion
SALAD

Daniel Boulud knows a thing or two about sausage, having grown up on his family's farm near Lyon, France, one of Europe's sausage-making capitals. Today, Boulud is one of America's most accomplished chefs, with award-winning restaurants in New York, Palm Beach, and Las Vegas, including the venerable Daniel. He still enjoys eating sausage, especially when presented in this simply elegant salad that he adapted from his restaurants for use in this book.

Almond oil is available in gourmet-food shops. If you can't locate it in your area, substitute olive oil. SERVES 4

2 tablespoons red wine
  vinegar
4 tablespoons almond oil
Salt
Freshly ground black pepper
8 small russet potatoes,
  unpeeled
2 Johnsonville Original
  Bratwurst Links
1/4 cup thinly sliced red
  onion
1/4 cup sliced almonds,
  toasted
1 tablespoon drained capers
1 tablespoon coarsely
  chopped fresh flat-leaf
  parsley
2 teaspoons coarsely
  chopped fresh tarragon
  leaves

1. To make the vinaigrette: Whisk together the vinegar and almond oil. Season to taste with salt and pepper.

2. To make the salad: Prepare the links according to package instructions. Slice into 1/4-inch coins.

3. Boil potatoes until tender. Drain, and allow to cool slightly. Cut into 1/4-inch thick slices. Set aside.

4. Place the sausage coins, onion, almonds, capers, parsley, tarragon, and potatoes in a large bowl. Add the vinaigrette, and toss well to coat. Adjust the seasoning with salt and pepper if necessary.

Johnsonville by the Numbers

7	Number of Johnsonville team members in 1965
1,000	Number of Johnsonville team members today
1.25	Number of times that, if laid end to end, all the Johnsonville brats sold per year would circle the globe
750	Number of Johnsonville brats that can be cooked on the Big Taste Grill at once
40	Number of countries in which Johnsonville sausage is sold
2,000,000	Number of dollars the Big Taste Grill has raised for charitable organizations in the past 9 years
54,000	Number of pounds each of the 65-foot Johnsonville Big Taste Grills weighs

Johnsonville's landscape has changed little since the founding of the Johnsonville Meat Market in 1945.

Warm Cajun
POTATO SALAD

We love this dish as an accompaniment to grilled Johnsonville sausage, but it also makes a tasty addition to a more formal plated dinner of steak, broiled fish, or chicken. SERVES 10

$1/4$ cup apple cider vinegar

$1/4$ cup sugar

One 16-ounce package Johnsonville New Orleans–Style Smoked Sausage

$1/8$ cup olive oil

$1/2$ bunch scallions, white parts only, sliced

$1/2$ red bell pepper, diced

$1/2$ green bell pepper, diced

$1/2$ teaspoon crushed garlic

All-purpose flour

$1/8$ cup Cajun seasoning

5 pounds red-skinned potatoes, peeled, boiled, and sliced

1. Preheat the oven to 350°F.

2. Bring $2^1/2$ cups water to a gentle boil in a large saucepan. Add the vinegar and sugar, and return to a gentle boil.

3. Pan-heat the sausage according to the package instructions. Coin-slice the sausage; reserve the pan and the juices.

4. Heat the pan and the juices over medium heat. Add the oil, scallions, red bell pepper, green bell pepper, and garlic, and sauté until the peppers are softened, about 3 minutes. Reserving the pan and any remaining liquid, remove the vegetables and transfer them to a bowl.

5. Whisk in just enough flour to absorb the liquid remaining in the pan. Cook over medium heat until lightly golden. Whisk in the water-vinegar mixture and the Cajun seasoning. Cook until the flour taste is cooked out and the sauce thickens to the consistency of honey, 8 to 10 minutes.

An early Big Taste Grill appearance. Today, the Big Taste Grill boasts a top grillin' speed of 2,500 bpm (brats per minute).

6. Place the potatoes in a large baking dish. Add the sausage and vegetables. Pour the thickened liquid over the mixture. Bake for 35 minutes, or until hot.

Salads and Sides

Summer Pasta Salad

You may serve this simple salad immediately, or chill it for an hour to allow the flavors to reach their peak. SERVES 6 TO 8

1 pound uncooked penne
   pasta
One 12-ounce package
   Johnsonville Garlic
   Summer Sausage, julienned
1 tomato, diced
1 red bell pepper, diced
1 green bell pepper, diced
1 cup snow peas, trimmed,
   sliced in half crosswise
1 bunch scallions, white and
   green parts, sliced
6 ounces Monterey Jack
   cheese, cubed
6 ounces extra-sharp
   Cheddar cheese, cubed
12 ounces Italian dressing
8 ounces balsamic
   vinaigrette

1. Cook the pasta according to the package instructions. Drain.

2. Place the pasta in a very large bowl. Add the sausage, tomato, red bell pepper, green bell pepper, snow peas, scallions, Monterey Jack cheese, Cheddar cheese, Italian dressing, and vinaigrette, and toss well to combine.

JOHNSONVILLE NEW ORLEANS–STYLE
Sausage with Beans and Apple

Sausage and beans have long enjoyed a tasty relationship, but never has the baked bean met the likes of our New Orleans–Style Smoked Sausage. With plump, juicy robustness that snaps back when you dig in, it's got a definite wild side. Tempered by the sweet-tartness of Granny Smith apples, this dish has just enough kick. SERVES 8 TO 10

Two 14-ounce cans baked
   beans
One 16-ounce package
   Johnsonville New
   Orleans–Style Smoked
   Sausage, bias-cut
4 Granny Smith apples,
   peeled, cored, and
   coarsely chopped
1/2 cup maple syrup
1/2 cup diced yellow onion
1 tablespoon Worcestershire
   sauce
1 teaspoon mustard powder
1/4 teaspoon salt
1/4 teaspoon freshly ground
   black pepper
2 garlic cloves, minced

1. Preheat the oven to 350°F.

2. Mix all ingredients in a large bowl. Place the mixture in a covered casserole dish. Bake, covered, for 2 hours. Remove the cover and bake an additional 20 minutes, until the juice thickens.

Salads and Sides

139

A 1990s Brat Days celebration.

Sausage, Pecan, and Cranberry
STUFFING

This moist and flavorful stuffing is a great side dish for the holiday season or anytime.

For added flavor, soak the cranberries in brandy or red wine for at least 1 hour or overnight. You may substitute large, unseasoned croutons for the day-old bread. SERVES 10 TO 12

Two 9-ounce packages Johnsonville Breakfast Patties

1 large yellow onion, coarsely chopped

1¹/₂ cups coarsely chopped celery

¹/₂ cup minced fresh parsley

2 garlic cloves, minced

12 cups coarsely chopped day-old bread

One 14-ounce can chicken broth

¹/₂ cup unsalted butter, melted

2 large eggs, lightly beaten

¹/₂ teaspoon rubbed sage

¹/₂ teaspoon dried thyme

¹/₂ teaspoon salt

¹/₂ teaspoon freshly ground black pepper

1 cup chopped pecans, toasted

1 cup dried cranberries

1. Preheat the oven to 350°F.

2. In a large skillet, cook and crumble the sausage over medium-high heat for 3 minutes. Add the onion and celery, and cook for 3 additional minutes, stirring occasionally. Add the parsley and garlic, and cook until the sausage is no longer pink and the vegetables are tender, 2 to 3 additional minutes. Drain and set aside.

3. Place the chopped bread in a large bowl. In a medium bowl, combine the broth, butter, eggs, sage, thyme, salt, and pepper. Pour this mixture over the bread; toss to coat. Fold in the pecans, cranberries, and sausage-vegetable mixture.

4. Spoon the stuffing into a greased 19-by-13-by-2-inch baking dish. Bake, uncovered, for 40 to 45 minutes, until it is golden brown and a thermometer inserted in the center reads 160°F.

—— GRANDMA ALICE'S *Sausage* STUFFING ——

Like her infectious laugh and youthful exuberance, Alice Stayer's coveted sausage-stuffing recipe has been a Johnsonville standby for the past 60 years. One taste of this moist, flavorful dish and you'll agree that it is bound to become one of her greatest legacies.

MAKES ENOUGH FOR A 7- TO 9-POUND BIRD

7 hard rolls (see page 151),
    cut into cubes
$1/2$ cup milk
One 19.76-ounce package
    Johnsonville Original
    Bratwurst Links, casings
    removed
$1/2$ cup diced yellow onion
1 cup diced celery
$1/4$ teaspoon freshly ground
    black pepper
$1/4$ teaspoon rubbed sage
$1/2$ teaspoon salt

1. Place the hard-roll cubes in a large bowl. Pour the milk over the cubes.

2. In a large skillet, cook and crumble the sausage over high heat until browned, 15 to 20 minutes. Reserve the drippings in the pan. Add the bratwurst to the bread-milk mixture.

3. In the same pan in which you browned the sausage, sauté the onion and celery in the bratwurst drippings. Add the onion, celery, pepper, and drippings to the sausage-bread mixture. Add the sage and salt, and mix well to combine. Stuff into the cavity of your bird of choice, and roast until golden brown and a thermometer inserted in the stuffing reads 160°F.

—— BEDDAR WITH *Cheddar* VEGETABLE BAKE ——

This is one of the most simple but satisfying recipes you'll ever make.

SERVES 6 TO 8

Two 16-ounce packages
    Johnsonville Beddar with
    Cheddar, cut into $1/2$-inch
    coins
Two 16-ounce packages
    California-blend frozen
    vegetables, thawed
One 16-ounce jar cheese
    sauce
One 16.3-ounce cylinder
    refrigerated buttermilk
    biscuits
1 cup shredded Cheddar
    cheese

1. Preheat the oven to 350°F.

2. Place the sausage coins in a 9-by-13-inch baking dish. Add the vegetables and cheese sauce; mix well.

3. Separate the biscuits, and arrange them over the vegetables and cheese. Sprinkle with cheese.

4. Bake for 20 to 30 minutes, until the center is hot and the biscuits are golden brown.

── ITALIAN AU GRATIN *potato* BAKE ──

Though Italian au Gratin Potato Bake is an excellent side dish for chicken, beef, pork roast, or even baked fish, it is substantial enough to be presented as a main course. For further comfort-food appeal, try mashing the potatoes. SERVES 6 TO 8

One 19.76-ounce package Johnsonville Mild Italian Links, casings removed
One 16-ounce package Velveeta cheese, cut into cubes
1 cup thick and chunky salsa
1¹/₂ teaspoons dried fennel seed
¹/₂ teaspoon dried aniseed
2 garlic cloves, minced
¹/₄ teaspoon dried basil
2 pounds russet potatoes, peeled, boiled, and sliced

1. Preheat the oven to 350°F.

2. In a large skillet, cook and crumble the sausage over medium heat until browned, 8 to 10 minutes. Drain.

3. Place the cheese, salsa, fennel seed, aniseed, garlic, and basil in a very large microwave-safe bowl, and microwave, stirring occasionally, on medium power until the cheese is melted. Add the sausage to this mixture. Microwave an additional 2 minutes on medium power, or until heated through.

4. Place the potatoes into a greased 9-by-13-inch baking dish. Pour the sausage-cheese mixture over the potatoes, and mix to combine. Bake for 35 minutes, or until golden brown.

CREOLE *Sausage* AND RICE

With onion, tomatoes, bell pepper, and the robust flavor of our Hot 'n Spicy Bratwurst, this tantalizing side dish has just enough heat. It's excellent served with chicken, or, for a more casual presentation, Johnsonville Natural Casing Wieners. SERVES 6

One 19.76-ounce package
   Johnsonville Hot 'n Spicy
   Bratwurst
1 teaspoon olive oil
1 large yellow onion, coarsely
   chopped
8 Roma tomatoes, chopped
$3/4$ cup coarsely chopped
   red bell pepper
$3/4$ cup coarsely chopped
   yellow bell pepper
$3/4$ cup coarsely chopped
   green bell pepper
$1/2$ teaspoon dried thyme
3 cups cooked long-grain
   rice, warm

1. Prepare the sausage according to the package instructions, and bias-slice.

2. Heat the oil in a large saucepan. Add the onion, and cook until glossy, 2 to 3 minutes. Add the tomatoes, and cook 5 additional minutes.

3. Add the red bell pepper, yellow bell pepper, green bell pepper, sausage, and thyme. Cook until the peppers are tender-crisp, 3 to 4 minutes. Serve over the rice.

Cajun Stuffed Peppers

This colorful recipe provides a delicious burst of flavor in every forkful. You may use the bell peppers of your choice, but a mixture of red, yellow, and green provides the most eye-dazzling pop. SERVES 6

Two 19.76-ounce packages Johnsonville Hot 'n Spicy Bratwurst, casings removed
2 cups cubed French bread
2 cups mixed frozen vegetables, thawed
Two 8-ounce cans tomato sauce
4 teaspoons Cajun seasoning
6 bell peppers

1. Preheat the oven to 425°F.

2. In a very large skillet, cook and crumble the sausage over high heat until just cooked through, 8 to 10 minutes. Drain.

3. In a medium bowl, combine the sausage, bread, vegetables, tomato sauce, and seasoning.

4. Cut the stems and top third off the peppers. With a small spoon, scoop out the seeds and membranes.

5. Fill each pepper with the sausage mixture, and place in a 9-by-13-inch baking pan. Add $1/4$ cup of water to the bottom of the pan. Cover, and bake for 30 to 35 minutes, until hot. Serve immediately.

Holyland Beans

For 10 years, Shelly resided in the quaint Wisconsin region known as the Holyland. With rolling hills dotted with red barns and church steeples for as far as one can see, the Holyland is home to villages like St. Cloud, St. Peter, and Mount Calvary. It's a place where life is just a bit slower, where families and friends still gather around the table for Sunday supper. Shelly adapted this recipe from the Wagner family of St. Joe, and no Johnsonville gathering would be complete without it.

Holyland Beans are best prepared a day in advance, to give all the flavors time to mingle. If you like your beans extra thick, add some cornstarch slurry or a roux—equal parts flour and fat—making sure to simmer for at least 10 to 15 minutes to cook out all the flour taste before serving. SERVES 16 TO 20

$2\frac{1}{2}$ tablespoons unsalted butter

$2\frac{1}{2}$ pounds Johnsonville Bratwurst Burger

1 cup diced yellow onion

Two $10\frac{3}{4}$-ounce cans condensed tomato soup

$1\frac{1}{2}$ cups packed brown sugar

4 tablespoons molasses

3 tablespoons ketchup

Four 28-ounce cans baked beans

1. Heat the butter in a very large saucepan over high heat. Add the burger and onion, and brown for 20 minutes. Drain. Return to low heat.

2. Add the soup, brown sugar, molasses, ketchup, and beans, and simmer, stirring frequently, for 45 minutes, or until thick and dark brown.

GRILLING
and *Tailgating*

TRADITIONAL SHEBOYGAN DOUBLE BRAT

REUBEN BRAT

PHILLY BRAT

TEXAN BBQ BRAT

CHILI BRATS

ITALIAN MEATBALL HOAGIE

TEX-MEX BRAT HOAGIE

STADIUM STYLE CONFETTI HOAGIE

OKTOBERFEST HOAGIE

SUMMER TURKEY HOAGIE

ITALIAN ONION AND BLUE CHEESE HOAGIE

CHIPOTLE SHRIMP, NEW ORLEANS–STYLE SAUSAGE,
AND PINEAPPLE SKEWERS

BRAT KEBABS

TEQUILA LIME AND VEGETABLE BRAT TAILGATE

SUMMER SAUSAGE S'MORES

*Sheboygan's first Brat Days
Parade was held in 1953.*

—TRADITIONAL *Sheboygan* DOUBLE BRAT—

This is the recipe that started it all, and if you look at the pair of juicy sausages on the cover of this book, is there any question why?

For greater ease, use Johnsonville Heat & Serve Brats, which pack all the great taste of our original bratwurst into a convenient, fully cooked link. MAKES 6 SANDWICHES

12 Johnsonville Original Bratwurst Links
6 round hard rolls (see sidebar), sliced open
Coarse-ground German-style mustard
1 large Vidalia onion, thinly sliced
Dill pickle slices

Grill the links according to the package instructions. Place two links on each hard roll. Slather with mustard, and top with onion and pickle slices.

What Came First, the Hard Roll or the Brat?

For the past 150 years, the German bakers in Sheboygan have been making hard rolls, our version of the German *Kaisersemmel,* which is a large, hard-crusted roll. Because one bratwurst would get lost in a roll of this size, we use two, and consider the sausage that slightly overhangs the edge an appetizer.

There is great local debate over which came first, the hard roll requiring two brats, or two brats that needed a large roll. You can guess our position.

If you can't find hard rolls, you may substitute kaiser rolls.

Da Werks: Brat Eating Do's and Don'ts

Sheboygan County, Wisconsin, is a German community known as the Brat Capital of the World. Here the famous double brat with the works is affectionately known as a "dubl brat wit' da werks"—said in a purposefully exaggerated Bavarian dialect.

Sheboygan County makes 75 percent of America's bratwurst, and if you want to eat like a local, you've got to learn our double-brat do's and don'ts:

- DO eat mustard on a double brat. Purists say the mustard should be Düsseldorf or another spicy brown mustard, such as stone-ground or even Dijon.

- DON'T serve a double brat on a flimsy hot-dog bun. It's simply not up to the honor. If you don't have hard rolls in your area, eat them on a kaiser roll. We'll forgive you.

- DO try to find bratwursts made in Sheboygan County. The sad, anemic-looking sausages hawked at ball games in some unfortunate cities quite literally pale in comparison.

- DON'T put sauerkraut on a double brat. It's a dead giveaway that you're not from round these parts and may result in not-so-good-natured ribbing.

- DO pair your double brat with beer, known locally as "bratwash." If the Good Lord wanted us to drink something fancy with our double brats, He'd have created a bratini.

- DON'T eat your double brat with a knife and fork. No pinkies poised in the air, either. That's just asking for trouble.

Reuben Brat

Though both New York and Omaha claim to be home of the famous Reuben sandwich, Johnsonville is the undisputed Reuben Brat capital of the world. Piled high with kraut, onion, and Thousand Island dressing, this sandwich is sure to please.

If you can't find dark-rye hoagie rolls, you may wish to substitute a pumpernickel, wheat, or sub roll. **MAKES 5 SANDWICHES**

One 19.76-ounce package Johnsonville Original Bratwurst Links
5 dark-rye hoagie rolls, hinge-sliced
1 tablespoon unsalted butter
1 large yellow onion, sliced
$1/3$ cup Thousand Island dressing
$1/3$ cup coarse-ground mustard
One 14-ounce can sauerkraut, drained

1. Grill the links according to the package instructions. Keep warm.

2. Place the rolls, cut side down, on the grill to toast lightly.

3. Melt the butter in a 9-by-13-inch aluminum-foil baking pan placed directly on the grill. Add the onion, and sauté until softened.

4. To make the Reuben sauce: Blend the dressing with the mustard. Spread the sauce over each open-face roll. Add the onion and one brat per roll. Top with the sauerkraut and serve immediately.

PHILLY
Brat

Philly cheese-steak lovers, meet your new best friend: the Philly Brat.

MAKES 5 SANDWICHES

2 tablespoons olive oil

1 large yellow onion, peeled and sliced

2 red bell peppers, cored, seeded, and sliced $1/4$ inch thick

2 yellow bell peppers, cored, seeded, and sliced $1/4$ inch thick

2 green bell peppers, cored, seeded, and sliced $1/4$ inch thick

Salt

Freshly ground black pepper

One 19.76-ounce package Johnsonville Original Bratwurst Links

5 ounces smoked provolone cheese

5 hoagie rolls, hinge-sliced

1. Heat the oil in a 9-by-13-inch aluminum-foil baking pan placed directly on the grill. Add the onion, red bell peppers, yellow bell peppers, and green bell peppers, and sauté until the peppers are softened. Season to taste with salt and pepper.

2. Grill the links according to the package instructions.

3. Place one slice of cheese on the bottom of each roll. Top with a link, onion, red bell pepper, yellow bell pepper, green bell pepper, and top of the roll.

Avoid the Dreaded Char Brat

It's a proud day when you graduate from hot dogs and burgers and grill your first Johnsonville brat. So don't ruin it by having the heat up too high or by sticking it with a meat fork. Slow-cooking a Johnsonville brat over medium heat is the key to its juicy goodness. And, sure, go ahead and poke a dog or a burger, but never puncture a Johnsonville brat. Ever. When you learn how to keep all that juicy flavor inside a brat until it's safely tucked away in your mouth, welcome to heaven on a bun. Welcome to Johnsonville.

— TEXAN *BBQ* BRAT —

Everything's bigger in Texas, but better with a Johnsonville brat. This new spin on the traditional BBQ sandwich is no exception. For an even easier preparation, use our delectable Heat & Serve Brats.

MAKES 5 SANDWICHES

One 19.76-ounce package
   Johnsonville Original
   Bratwurst Links
1/2 cup barbecue sauce
5 hoagie rolls, hinge-sliced
   and grilled
15 slices shaved ham
15 slices smoked Cheddar
   cheese
1 small red onion, peeled and
   sliced
1/2 cup salsa

1. Grill the links according to the package instructions. Keep warm.

2. Spread 1 teaspoon of the barbecue sauce on each side of each roll. Place three slices each of ham and cheese inside each roll. Add a bratwurst, and top with onion and salsa.

— CHILI *Brats* —

You've heard of the chili dog. Now meet its superior, the Chili Brat.

Two 19.76-ounce packages
  Johnsonville Original
  Bratwurst Links
2 tablespoons unsalted
  butter
$1/2$ cup diced red bell pepper
$1/2$ cup diced green bell
  pepper
1 cup diced yellow onion
$1^1/2$ pounds fresh ground
  beef
2 tablespoons cocoa powder
One 10-ounce can diced
  tomatoes with green chiles
One 16-ounce can chili beans
One $15^1/2$-ounce can Bush's
  Chili Magic Chili Starter
Ten 12-inch flour tortillas
1 cup shredded sharp
  Cheddar cheese

1. Grill the links according to the package instructions. Keep warm.

2. Melt the butter in a 9-by-13-inch aluminum-foil baking pan placed directly on the grill. Add the peppers, and sauté until tender. Add the onion, and cook until glossy.

3. Add the ground beef, and sprinkle with the cocoa powder. Brown until cooked through, about 5 minutes. Add the tomatoes, beans, and starter, and simmer for 15 minutes.

4. Heat the flour tortillas according to the package instructions. Place a bratwurst on one-half of each tortilla. Top with about $1/2$ cup of the meat mixture. Sprinkle with the cheese. Fold over the tortillas and serve.

Italian Meatball
HOAGIE

These saucy meatballs are fantastic served on their own as an hors d'oeuvre, or over pasta. Because they transport well, they're great for a tailgating party. Prepare them at home and simply reheat them in an aluminum-foil baking pan on the grill.

You may use Johnsonville Mild, Sweet, or Hot Italian Links in this recipe. SERVES 4 TO 6

2 large eggs, lightly beaten
$3/4$ cup bread crumbs
$1/4$ cup grated Romano
   cheese
$1/2$ teaspoon minced garlic
One 26-ounce jar marinara
   sauce
One 19.76-ounce package
   Johnsonville Italian Links,
   casings removed, or Italian
   Ground Sausage
6 hoagie rolls, hinge-sliced

1. Preheat the oven to 375°F.

2. In a large bowl, combine the eggs, bread crumbs, cheese, garlic, and $1/2$ cup of the marinara sauce. Let stand until all the liquid is absorbed, 3 to 5 minutes.

3. Add the sausage to this mixture. Using your hands, mix well to combine. Roll into golf-ball-size meatballs. Place on a rimmed baking sheet, and bake for 15 to 20 minutes, or until the internal temperature of the meatballs is 180°F. Drain.

4. Meanwhile, heat the remaining marinara sauce in a large saucepan over medium heat. Add the meatballs, and stir to coat completely.

5. Place 3 to 4 meatballs with sauce on each roll, and serve immediately.

Tex-Mex Brat

HOAGIE

A burst of Tex-Mex flavor explodes in every bite of this saucy sandwich.

MAKES 5 SANDWICHES

One 19.76-ounce package
   Johnsonville Original
   Bratwurst Links
$1/2$ cup barbecue sauce
5 hoagie rolls, hinge-sliced
10 thin slices ham
10 thin slices smoked
   Cheddar cheese
1 small red onion, sliced
$1/2$ cup salsa

1. Grill the links according to the package instructions. Keep warm.

2. Spread the barbecue sauce on the inside of each roll. Place 2 slices each of ham and cheese inside a roll. Top with a link. Cover with some onion and salsa. Repeat with remaining rolls.

Johnsonville Sausage Executive Chef Michael Zeller and PBS host Steven Raichlen with the Big Taste Grill.

Grilling and Tailgating

The Brat Tub: How to Keep Sausage Hot and Juicy

No self-respecting grillmeister serves brats that have overstayed their welcome on the grill. One sure-fire way to see that all your guests get a piping-hot, juicy Johnsonville brat is to create a simple bratwurst hot tub. You'll need one 8-by-4$\frac{1}{2}$-inch aluminum-foil baking pan per dozen brats.

3 cans beer
2 tablespoons unsalted butter
1 small yellow onion, sliced

1. Heat the grill.

2. Pour the beers into a pan directly on the grill, and add the butter and onions.

3. Grill your Johnsonville brats to a juicy, golden-brown perfection. Serve immediately, or place any remaining brats into the steaming hot tub. When folks are ready for seconds or thirds—or when stragglers show up late—grab a Johnsonville brat out of the tub and let them enjoy.

Confetti Hoagie

These sandwiches look festive, and after just one bite there'll be a veritable party in your mouth. SERVES 6

One 16-ounce package
  Johnsonville Stadium Style
  Brats
6 hoagie rolls, hinge-sliced
12 slices Swiss cheese
4 cups finely shredded
  cabbage
1 cup finely chopped red
  onion
1 cup finely chopped green
  bell pepper
$3/4$ cup Russian dressing

1. Heat the grill.

2. Prepare the brats according to the package instructions. Open the rolls; place a brat on each roll and leave open. Top with the cheese.

3. Grill or broil the hoagies until the cheese melts, watching carefully so they don't burn.

4. In a large bowl, combine the cabbage, onion, pepper, and dressing. Spoon this mixture over the hoagies. Top each with 2 slices of cheese and serve the sandwiches open-faced.

—— OKTOBERFEST *Hoagie* ——

With these hearty hoagies, we once again call on Wisconsin's rich German heritage. Though they're quite substantial, they're also absolutely delicious, so you may want to make extra while you're at it.

MAKES 5 SANDWICHES

One 19.76-ounce package
  Johnsonville Original
  Bratwurst Links
2 tablespoons horseradish
  sauce
5 hoagie rolls, hinge-sliced
5 ounces shaved roast turkey
5 ounces shaved ham
2 medium tomatoes, sliced
10 thin slices provolone
  cheese
10 slices bacon, cooked crisp
  and drained
2 small yellow onions, sliced
5 slices dill pickle
1 1/2 cups shredded lettuce

1. Grill the links according to the package instructions. Let cool slightly; hinge-cut in half lengthwise.

2. Spread horseradish sauce on the inside of each bun. Add one split bratwurst per bun. Top with the turkey, ham, tomatoes, cheese, bacon, onions, pickle slices, and lettuce.

Preventing Flare-Up

You've got a grill full of Johnsonville brats, then it happens: the flare-up. Don't panic. First, move the brats to safety. Second, cool those coals. Quick action now will keep all that juicy flavor inside, where it belongs. If you don't have a water bottle available, we regret to inform you you'll be forced to take desperate measures. You're going to have to temper those flames with that beer you're holding. The day you learn that being a hero doesn't come without a price, you're one step closer to becoming a grillmeister.

The Johnsonville Big Taste Grill appears at more than 1,000 events per year.

— SUMMER *Turkey* HOAGIE —

Any of our precooked delicious Summer Sausage varieties would work in this recipe: Original, Beef, Garlic, or Old World. SERVES 2

One 10-inch loaf French
  bread
4 tablespoons creamy garlic
  dressing
3 leaves romaine lettuce
Three $1/8$-inch-thick slices
  turkey breast
Seven $1/8$-inch-thick slices
  Johnsonville Summer
  Sausage
One $1/8$-inch-thick slice red
  onion, rings separated
Five $1/8$-inch-thick slices
  tomato
Four $1/8$-inch-thick slices
  extra-sharp Cheddar
  cheese

Slice the bread in half lengthwise. Spread both pieces with the dressing. Layer one piece with lettuce, turkey, sausage, onion, tomato, and cheese. Top with the other piece. Slice in half.

—ITALIAN ONION AND *Blue Cheese* HOAGIE—

Elegant enough for a backyard baby shower but hearty enough for a tailgate party at Green Bay's Lambeau Field, this sandwich packs unexpected flavor. MAKES 6 SANDWICHES

1 medium yellow onion, thinly sliced

4 ounces blue cheese, crumbled

2 tablespoons red wine vinegar

1 teaspoon chopped fresh chives

1 teaspoon chopped fresh parsley

$1/2$ teaspoon minced garlic

1 tablespoon steak sauce

$1/4$ teaspoon salt

$1/4$ teaspoon freshly ground black pepper

$1/4$ cup olive oil

One 19.76-ounce package Johnsonville Mild Italian Links

6 hoagie rolls, hinge-sliced

1. Heat the grill.

2. To make the dressing: In a large bowl, whisk together the onion, cheese, vinegar, chives, parsley, garlic, steak sauce, salt, and pepper. Whisking constantly, add the oil in a thin, steady stream.

3. To make the sandwich: Grill the links according to the package instructions. Place a link on the bottom of each roll, and top with the dressing. For added texture, place the sandwiches open-faced on the grill or under the broiler until the cheese melts. Close the sandwiches, and serve immediately.

The Self-Respecting Grillmeister's Tools of the Brat Grilling Trade

Gas or Charcoal Grill

The choice is up to you. Purists prefer charcoal grills for smoke-infused flavor. But it's hard to beat a gas grill for convenience. Many serious grillers have both—a gas grill for "home" cookouts, and a charcoal grill for tailgating, camping, and grilling on the road.

Grilling Tongs

When you pierce Johnsonville brats with a meat fork, aka a cattle prod, all those flavorful juices will escape. Always use grilling tongs. The best are spring-loaded, with a handle at least 16 inches long to keep you away from the heat.

Water Bottle

Flare-ups happen to the best of us. The key is to be ready and knock down those flames before they cause the dreaded char brat. A squirt from a water bottle will do the trick.

Grilling Apron or Towel

Grilling's a dirty job, but someone's got to do it. And though your jeans are a fine place to wipe your hands in some circles, you may want to don a goofy apron or simply have a kitchen towel or two within reach.

Serving Tray

No one wants to eat dry, overcooked brats—or ones served from the same plate that delivered them to the grill in their raw state. When they are grilled to perfection, platter up your delicacies on a clean serving tray and watch your guests dig in.

The Brat Tub

The brat tub (see page 160) is a great way to hold extra brats until they're ready to be enjoyed.

Cooler

It's hard to concentrate on grilling and bartending at the same time, so make your party a self-serve affair. Fill a cooler with assorted beverages and ice, and let the good times roll.

CHIPOTLE SHRIMP,
New Orleans–Style Sausage,
AND PINEAPPLE SKEWERS

Chef Mike Zeller has gotten used to bringing these zesty, eye-popping skewers to every gathering with his Johnsonville co-workers. No one can seem to get enough of them, and after just one bite, you'll see why.

Though we've presented the skewers over rice, you could place them on a bed of lightly buttered linguine drizzled with the sauce. Johnsonville Hot 'n Spicy Bratwurst or Hot Italian Links work great in place of the New Orleans–Style Smoked Sausage.

You will need ten skewers for this recipe. Soak wooden skewers in water for 30 minutes before use. For added zip, add a few dashes of Tabasco Chipotle Pepper Sauce to the water. MAKES 10 SKEWERS

SKEWERS
One 16-ounce package Johnsonville New Orleans–Style Smoked Sausage
1 pound jumbo shrimp, peeled and deveined
10 ounces pineapple chunks
5 tablespoons Tabasco Chipotle Pepper Sauce

SAUCE
2 tablespoons olive oil
4 garlic cloves, minced
$3/4$ cup sour cream
$1/4$ cup pineapple juice
3 tablespoons lime juice

DISH
$2^1/2$ cups cooked long-grain rice, warm
3 tablespoons chopped fresh cilantro

1. Heat the grill.

2. To make the skewers: Cut each sausage into six equal chunks.

3. Skewer a piece of sausage through the casing. Add a shrimp and then a piece of pineapple. Repeat twice per skewer.

4. Place the skewers on a large plate, and brush with the pepper sauce.

*Johnsonville brats are the
favorite of young and old.*

5. To make the sauce: Pour the oil in a large sauté pan, and heat over medium heat. Add the garlic, and sauté for 1 minute. Add the sour cream, pineapple juice, and lime juice, and simmer for 5 to 7 minutes, until thickened.

6. Grill the skewers for 3 minutes. Flip and grill an additional 3 minutes. Serve the skewers over the rice. Top with the sauce and the cilantro.

Oops! Your Sausage Is Showing!

Ever create neat-looking sausage skewers, only to have them warp and ooze from their casings while on the grill? When preparing a recipe like kebabs that calls for sliced raw sausage, partially freeze the sausage beforehand. When the sausage is frozen but thawed enough so that it can be bent slightly, it will give you a clean slice. This technique also prevents the sausage from losing its shape or oozing.

BRAT *Kebabs*

When grilling and tailgating, we use a lot of bag marinades. Marinating items in a resealable plastic bag is not only easy for transport but great for allowing the marinade to work its way into whatever you're marinating. Plus, the airtight seal ensures that all the delicious flavor and aroma stay inside. Try it next time you grill. SERVES 4 TO 6

$^1/_2$ cup soy sauce

$^1/_4$ cup frozen apple-juice concentrate, thawed

3 tablespoons spicy mustard

2 red bell peppers, cut into 1-inch pieces

1 yellow bell pepper, cut into 1-inch pieces

1 green bell pepper, cut into 1-inch pieces

1 medium onion, cut into wedges

2 Granny Smith apples, cored and cut into 1-inch cubes

1 medium yellow squash, cut into 1-inch cubes

One 16-ounce package Johnsonville Smoked Bratwurst, frozen and sliced into 1-inch chunks

1. To make the marinade: Place the soy sauce, juice, and mustard in a resealable plastic bag, and seal completely. Shake gently to combine. Add the red bell peppers, yellow bell pepper, green bell pepper, onion, apples, and squash. Refrigerate for 1 hour to allow the flavors to infuse. Remove the vegetables and fruit from the marinade, and reserve both.

2. Heat the grill.

3. To make the kebabs: Alternately spear the sausage through the casings, the red bell peppers, yellow bell pepper, green bell pepper, onion, apples, and squash with the skewers. Brush with the reserved marinade.

4. Grill over medium-hot coals, turning and brushing with additional marinade often, until the sausage is hot and the vegetables and fruit are cooked through, 15 to 20 minutes. Serve immediately.

TEQUILA LIME AND VEGETABLE
Brat Tailgate

Bored with burgers? This tailgate is sure to shake things up. Topped with tender marinated vegetables, juicy Johnsonville brats are a winner before the game even starts.

If you can't locate tequila-lime marinade in your area, use the tequila of your choice and sprinkle the finished dish with fresh lime juice. SERVES 10

---

1 medium eggplant, cut lengthwise into $^1/_2$-inch-thick slices

12 scallions, white and green parts, sliced

2 large beefsteak tomatoes, cut into $^1/_2$-inch-thick slices

One 16-ounce bottle tequila-lime marinade

2 large red-skinned potatoes, cut into $^1/_4$-inch-thick slices

2 tablespoons crushed garlic

$^1/_2$ cup olive oil

Salt

Freshly ground black pepper

Two 19.76-ounce packages Johnsonville Original Bratwurst Links

---

1. Place the eggplant, scallions, tomatoes, and marinade in a 1-gallon resealable storage bag. Shake the bag to coat the vegetables completely with the marinade. Marinate for at least 1 hour and up to 24 hours in the refrigerator or cooler.

2. In a second 1-gallon resealable storage bag, place the potatoes, garlic, oil, and salt and pepper to taste. Marinate for at least 1 hour and up to 24 hours in the refrigerator or cooler.

3. Heat the grill.

4. Grill the links according to the package instructions. Keep warm.

5. Place the contents of both bags on the grill, discarding the marinades, and cook to your desired doneness. Serve the bratwursts topped with the marinated vegetables.

Tailgating Do's and Don'ts

- DO get to the game early to claim your turf. More than 50 percent of tailgaters set up more than 3 hours before the game.

- DON'T forget to bring along your rain gear. When others are huddled in their vehicles, you'll be grilling up juicy Johnsonville brats.

- DO look the part. Whether it's a cheesehead hat or team colors on you or your rig, you should show your team loyalty and show the opposing fans whose turf they're grilling on.

- DON'T forget to bring along chairs. You need all your energy for inside the stadium and shouldn't expend it standing over the grill.

— SUMMER *Sausage* S'MORES —

These are a crowd favorite at Johnsonville cooking demonstrations nationwide. Kids love them, and they're great for meals on the go.

Summer Sausage S'Mores may be served hot off the grill or at room temperature—if they last that long! SERVES 6

Six ¼-inch-thick slices
  Johnsonville Summer
  Sausage
6 slices Cheddar cheese, cut
  to diameter of sausage
12 round crackers
¼ cup coarse-ground
  mustard

1. Place the sausage slices on a hot grill. Cook until the sausages start to cup, about 3 minutes. Flip the sausages, and place the cheese inside the cupped side. Cover the grill, and allow the cheese to melt.

2. Spread the crackers with a thin layer of mustard.

3. Remove the sausage cups from the grill, and sandwich them between the crackers just before serving.

Father and son, Ralph F. Stayer and Ralph C. Stayer,
before the 2003 groundbreaking of the latest
Johnsonville Sausage facility.

INDEX

Index

Index

Index

Index

Index

Index

Index

Index

© Blue Moon Studios

SHELLY STAYER is the wife of Johnsonville owner and CEO Ralph Stayer and a co-owner of Sushi Samba in Chicago and Fusion Restaurant in Fond du Lac, Wisconsin. She attended the Culinary Institute of America, has three children, and lives in Fond du Lac and in New York City.

SHANNON KRING BIRÓ is the executive producer, writer, and costar of the Emmy® Award–winning PBS cooking series *The Kitchens of Biró*. She is the co-author of *Biró: European-Inspired Cuisine* and the forthcoming *Ó: SpanAsian Cuisine by Biró* and the author of *Sister Salty, Sister Sweet: A Memoir of Sibling Rivalry and Sisterhood.* She has been featured on NPR and in publications including *The Wall Street Journal, TV Guide, SmartMoney* magazine, *Redbook, Women's World,* and the *Chicago Tribune.* She lives in Miami and in Los Angeles.